TINKER WITH ELECTRONICS

(PART I – BASIC CIRCUITS)

Sunil Mathews

Printed and sold by *Notion Press Publishers*

INTRODUCTION

Welcome to the fascinating world of electronics! Have you ever wondered how your favorite gadgets work? Or how information travels from one device to another? We should thank the electronic circuits that works tirelessly behind the scenes to make all those possible.

Imagine a world without these circuits – no cool gadgets, no fun games! We rely on them more than we realize, whether it's chatting with friends on our phones or playing games on our tablets.

But did you know that these circuits have a fascinating history? They started way back in the 1800s with the invention of the telegraph, and since then, they've evolved into the amazing technology we have today.

Electronics is a vast and ever-evolving field, with new discoveries and innovations happening every day. At its core lies the humble electron, the tiny particle responsible for all the magic. Whether it's flowing through wires to create electrical currents, navigating resistors to regulate flow, or finding a home in capacitors to store charge, electrons are the work force behind every electronic device.

Think of electronic circuits like puzzles made up of thousands of tiny pieces. Each piece has a special job to do, like turning on a light or making a sound. And guess what? We're going to learn all about these pieces and how to put them together to create our very own gadgets!

But with such complexity, where do you even begin? Just like tackling any big task, learning electronics is all about taking it one step at a time. You don't need to master every aspect of electronics to start going. Instead, let's break it down into manageable pieces and focus on mastering the basics.

In this book, we'll embark on a journey through the fundamentals, familiarizing the students with symbols and simple circuit diagrams, exploring commonly used components and how they all come together to form a working circuit. From simple projects to more complex designs, we'll learn them all by doing, building our understanding one circuit at a time.

We don't want to make it another school session, where you start everything with an in depth understanding of theory and almost nil hands on! We will follow a contrary approach – No theory and full hands on!

So, whether you're a curious kid who is eager to explore the world of electronics or a teacher looking to inspire the next generation of innovators, get ready to dive into the world of electronics, where we'll explore the basics and then get creative building our own circuits. Who knows? Maybe you'll even invent the next big thing!

CONTENTS

TINY HEROES IN THE KIT

We need a toolkit to practice hands-on, don't we? Well, I've compiled a list of items — enough to dive into numerous simple yet interesting circuits as a beginner. The journey begins with powering up an LED quickly and progresses to crafting your own audio amplifier!

Every electronic gadget and gizmo is powered by thousands of tiny, mysterious components! Imagine a playground where these parts work in rhythm to bring our toys, games, and devices to life.

Depending on the gadget we use, there could be hundreds, thousands, or even millions of components, each playing its unique role perfectly in synchronization with others! Now, imagine yourself as the team manager, assigning each one a specific role to achieve our goal! You might be wondering how to tackle this mammoth task without knowing them well, right? Indeed, it's essential to have some basic knowledge about them to position them correctly on the playground!

But don't worry if it all seems a bit mysterious at first – you don't need to be a wizard to understand how it all works! We're about to embark on an adventure, starting by acquainting ourselves with some basic and special members of the vast family of the true heroes of electronics!

<u>**Light Emitting Diode**</u>

A Light Emitting Diode, or LED for short, is a tiny component that glows, when an electric current flows through it. LEDs have a multitude of practical applications. They're often used to indicate that the circuit is powered up, to signal that it's functioning as expected, or to warn you when something has gone amiss in your circuit. You can join several LEDs together to make large displays, or let your creativity shine by using them in decorative lighting arrangements.

LEDs are available in many sizes and shape and a wide array of colors, including red, green, blue, and many others. There is also a special type of LED known as RGB, where a red, green, and blue LED are integrated into a single package. These colors can be mixed, allowing you to create a diverse spectrum of different colors by adjusting the intensity of each of the three primary colors – Red, Green and Blue.

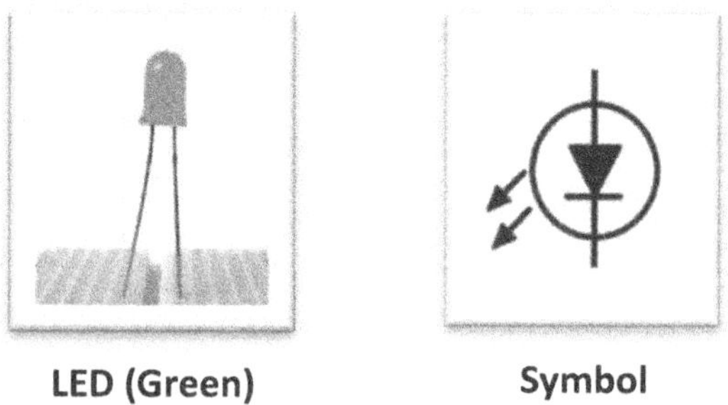

LED (Green)   **Symbol**

Symbols serve as representations for different components within a circuit. In the diagram above, you can spot a symbol used for LED.

LEDs are unidirectional devices, permitting electric current to flow in only one direction. Ensuring the correct connection is crucial: link the anode terminal to the positive end of the battery and the cathode to the negative end, to ensure your LED glows normally.

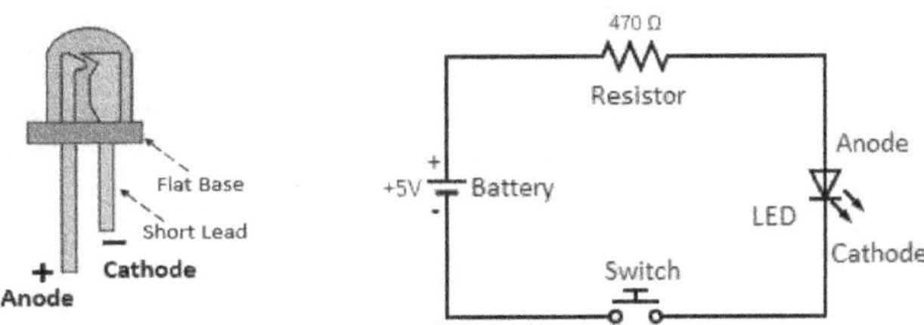

Fig. Identifying Terminals   *Fig. Circuit Diagram*

A brand new LED will have the Anode terminal a bit longer than the Cathode terminal. You can also identify the terminals, by looking for a tiny flat portion on the circular base. The terminal adjacent to that will be Cathode (-). You can also hold it against light and examine the terminals within the transparent shield. The lead that appears slightly smaller and almost straight corresponds to the Anode (+), while the one with a bit longer protrusion is the Cathode (-).

Note: Do not connect a LED directly to the battery. The operating current of an LED is very low (Safe operating range is 10 – 20 milli amperes), and a higher current could result in permanent damage to it. In order to limit the current, a resistor should always be connected in series with the LED, while connecting to the battery.

<u>Resistor</u>

A resistor introduces resistance into a circuit, restricting the flow of current in a circuit. Greater the resistance of a circuit, the lower the current that will pass through it.

Resistors are essential components in electronic circuits, enabling the use of a single supply voltage throughout the circuit by limiting the voltage at different points in the circuit.

The current in a circuit will be proportional to the applied voltage (Known as Ohms Law). It means, the ratio of voltage to current remains constant, which we refer as **resistance**. Unit of resistance is **Ohm** (Ω).

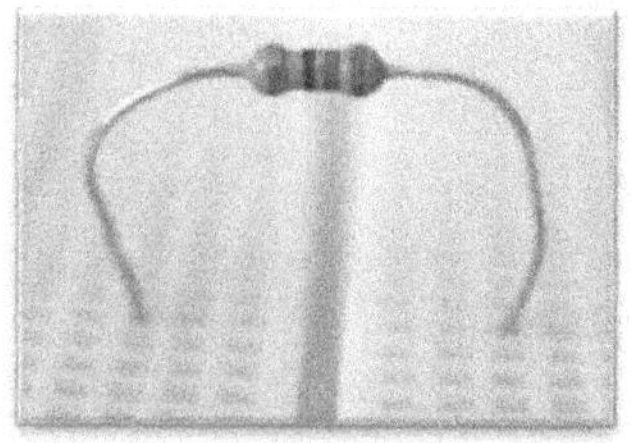

Resistor

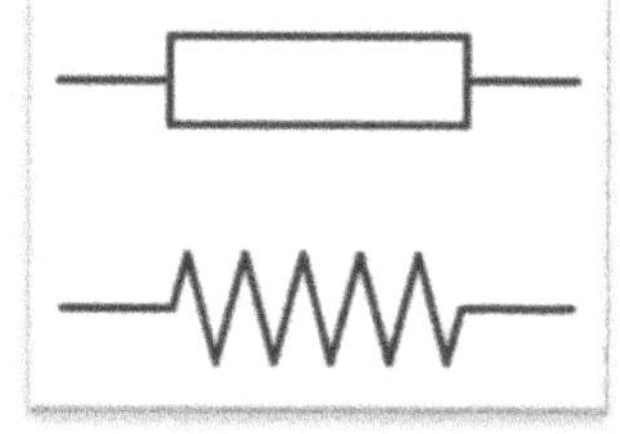

Symbol IEC/US Standards

Resistors are non-directional devices and have no polarity, meaning that interchanging the terminals would not have any effect on the circuit.

Value of carbon resistors are indicated by the colour codes printed on them.

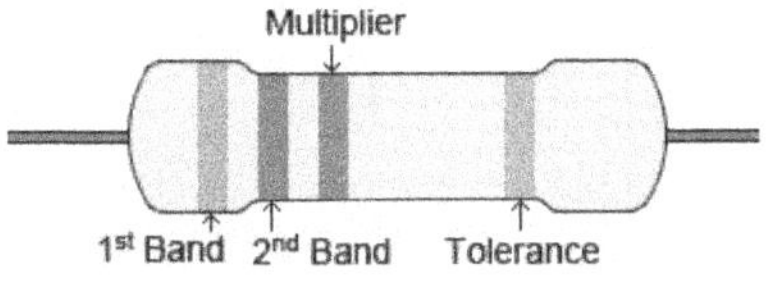

Color	1st, 2nd Band Significant Figures	Multiplier	Color	1st, 2nd Band Significant Figures	Multiplier
Black	0	× 1	Green	5	× 100K
Brown	1	× 10	Blue	6	× 1M
Red	2	× 100	Violet	7	× 10M
Orange	3	× 1K	Grey	8	× 100M
Yellow	4	× 10K	White	9	× 1G

Fig. Colour Code values

Write down the digits corresponding to the first two color bands and then append the corresponding number of zeros as indicated by the third color band. The result will represent the value of the resistor in Ohms. If the resulted value is too high, we express the value in Kilo Ohms (KΩ) or Mega Ohms (MΩ), where the value will be divided by 1000 & 1000000 respectively for easy denotation.

Examples:

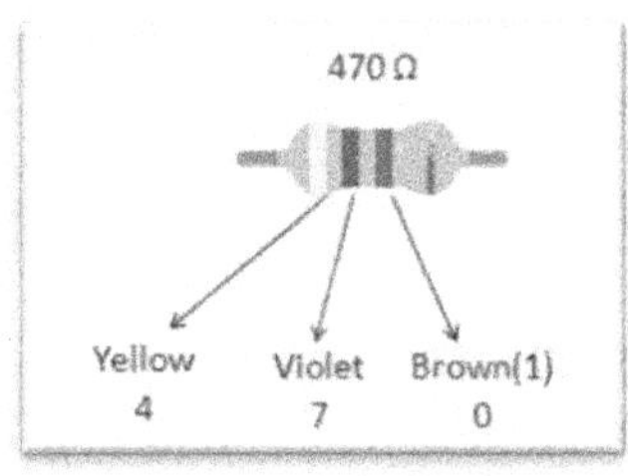

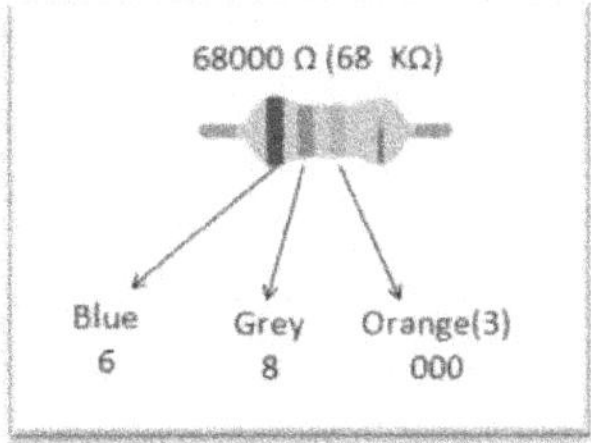

Value = 4 7 0 Ohms
or **470 Ohms**

Value = 6 8 000 Ohms
or **68 Kilo Ohms**

Capacitor

Capacitors behave like a battery with very low capacity, as it can store and release electric charge. Capacitors are often used to introduce a time delay in a circuit, by holding charge for a definite time. They are useful for removing noise from an audio signal or stabilizing the power supply of a circuit.

Capacitors come in polarized and non-polarized types. The primary distinction is that polarized capacitors have a positive and a negative pin, and it's essential to connect them correctly.

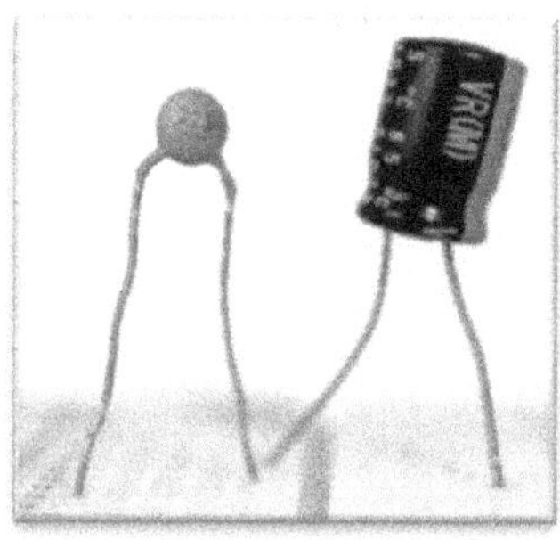

Capacitors

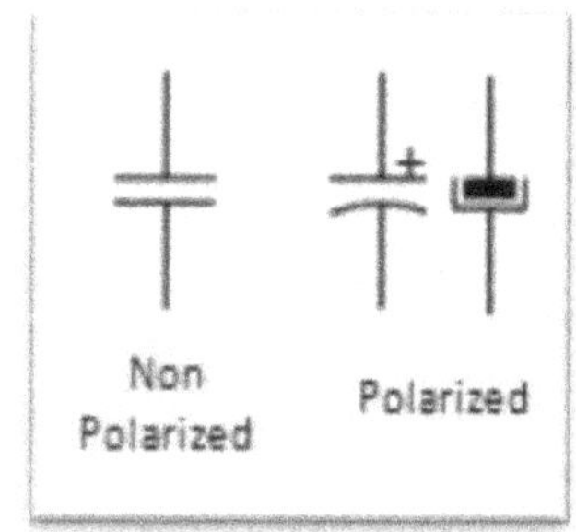

Capacitor - Symbols

Capacitors offer high resistance to low frequency signals and low resistance to high frequency signals. It can therefore block dc voltage, and offer a smooth passage to ac voltages. Unit of capacitance is Farad (F). In electronic circuits we often use less value capacitors of micro farads (µf) and pico farads (pf).

Polarized capacitors have positive and negative terminals, and are to be connected in the correct polarity when used in circuits.

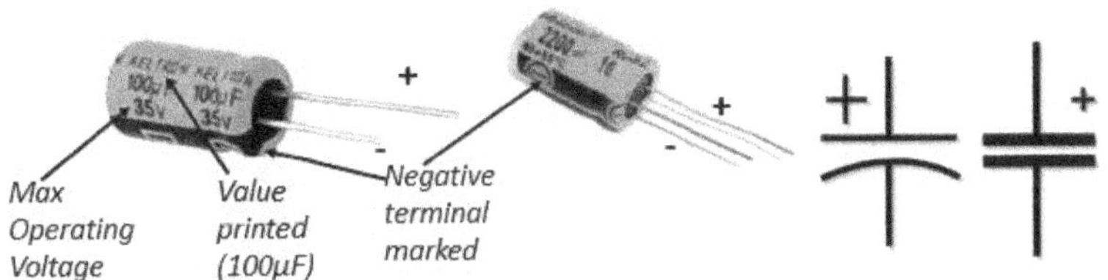

Fig – Finding the Value and identifying the terminals

A polarized capacitor may have an orange, black, blue or any other colour sleeve. The colour depends on the manufacturer and does not have any significance. Value of a polarized capacitor will be printed on the outer sleeve in µF as shown in the figure above. There will be a –ve marking on the sleeve, the terminal against that marking will be the negative terminal. The other terminal (away from the –ve marking) will be the positive terminal.

Non Polarized Capacitors

A non polarized capacitor could be in different colour and shape, depending on the manufacturer. It does not have polarity, which means that it could be connected without bothering about mixing up of the terminals in a circuit.

The value of the capacitor will be written in codes as shown in the figure below.

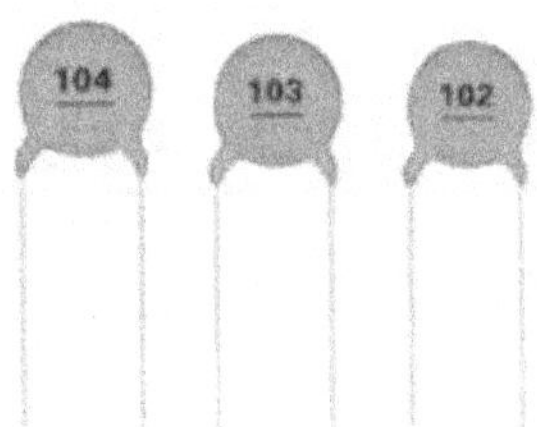

102 - Value **0.001 µF**.

103 - Value **0.01 µF**

104 - Value **0.1 µF**

Diode

Diodes are unidirectional devices, allowing current to flow in only one direction. They are an integral part of any rectifier circuit, converting AC signals into DC signals. In other words, they exhibit almost zero resistance when they are forward biased and infinite resistance in a reverse-biased state.

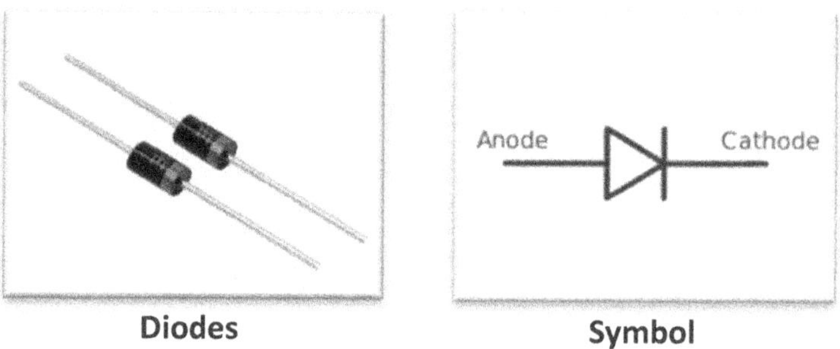

Diodes   **Symbol**

Diodes come in various shapes and sizes, serving distinct purposes depending on their intended applications. LED is also a type of diode that emits light when a current flows through it.

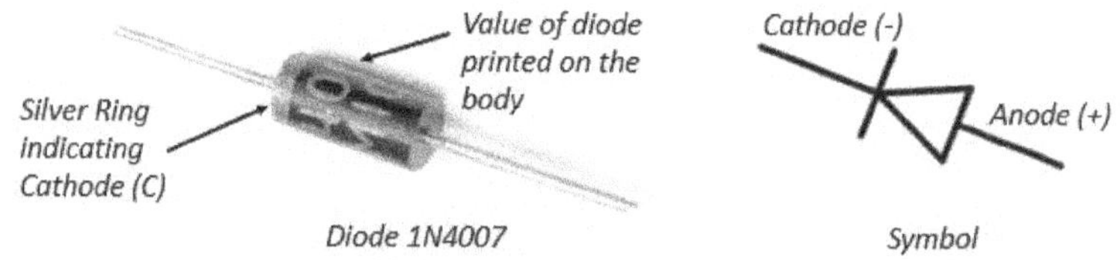

Diode 1N4007   Symbol

Fig. Finding Value & Identifying Cathode of a diode

Value of a diode will be printed on the outer body in a contrasting colour. Also, you can find a ring printed at one end on the body of the diode. The terminal on that end will be cathode (– ve). We should connect the positive voltage at the Anode, for the diode to allow the current to flow in the normal operation mode.

Transistor

A transistor has three pins named base, collector, and emitter. By controlling the voltage applied at the base terminal, the transistor can function like a two stage On/Off switch, making it useful in electronic triggering of circuits.

The transistor can also be made to conduct in a partially on state, by controlling the current that goes through its base. Based on the gain factor (varies from transistor to transistor), a small current applied at the base terminal can result in a larger collector current (ie. base current multiplied by the gain factor). Thus the transistor can also function like an amplifier.

Transistors

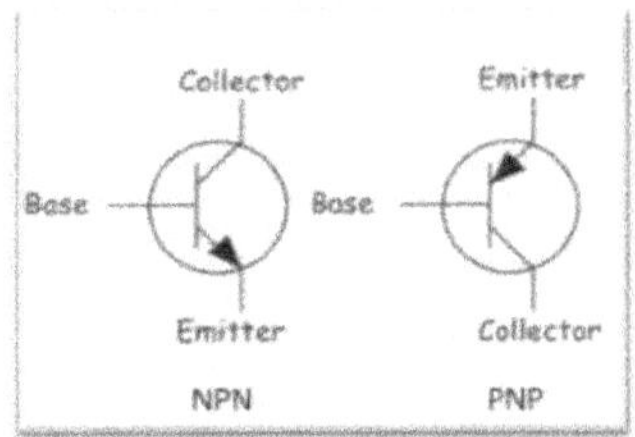

Symbols NPN & PNP Type

Bipolar Junction Transistors, which we will be dealing with right now, fall into two category ie. NPN and PNP, based on the internal construction. Both the types function identically, except voltages (Positive/Negative) applied on the terminals are complimentary to one another. A negative voltage at the base trigger a PNP transistor, whereas a positive voltage at the base triggers a NPN transistor.

There are many more types of transistors, each designed for specific purposes. As a beginner it is not essential to explore all those and we shall limit our discussion to the commonly used BJT transistors.

It is important to identify and connect the three pins of a transistor correctly. If they are inter changed, the transistor will not work, and may even end up damaging it.

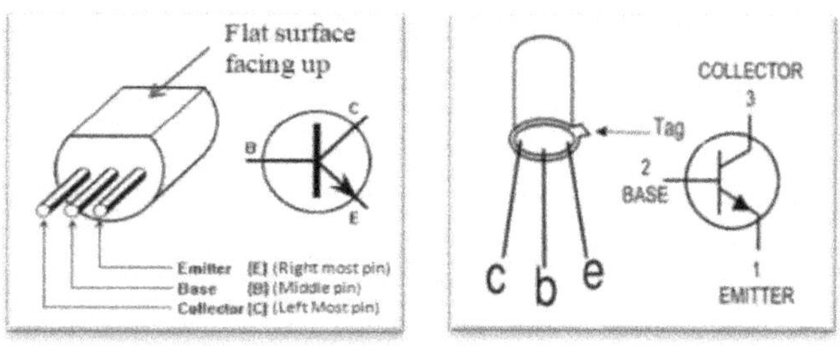

Fig. Identifying the Pins of a Transistor

Low power transistor packaging is made of plastic material having a characteristic surface that is flat, while those made of metal have a protrusion (tag) on the plate underneath.

For transistors with the flat face, hold the flat face upward facing the pins towards you as shown. The right most pin will be emitter, the middle one will be base and the left most will be collector.

For transistors with a small tag on the casing, the pin just next to the tag will be emitter, the one closer to the emitter will be base and the farthest from the emitter will be the collector pin.

Integrated Circuits

An integrated circuit (IC) is a type of circuit that is compactly integrated onto a semiconductor chip. It can serve various functions such as acting as a radio transmitter, a microcontroller, an audio amplifier, or virtually any other circuit imaginable. By condensing a circuit onto a small chip, it becomes significantly easier to create advanced projects.

For instance, let's say we want to create an intrusion monitoring system for our office. In this case, we can obtain chips designed for specific functions such as motion detection, light and sound sensing, and more. Additionally, you would need a GSM chip to transmit text messages and a microcontroller chip to manage all the device's operations. We can find detailed information about the specific functions and capabilities of these chips in their respective datasheets.

As a young electronics enthusiast, one should know two of the most commonly used ICs, ie. NE 555 Timer IC and LM 741 Op Amp Chip.

NE 555 Timer

The 555 timer is an exceptionally versatile and widely used integrated circuit. The standard 555 timer package includes 25 transistors, 2 diodes, and 15 resistors on a silicon chip installed in an 8-pin mini dual-in-line package.

It can be employed for various purposes, such as generating blinking light sequences, producing sound, creating clock signals, implementing countdown timers, and a wide range of other applications.

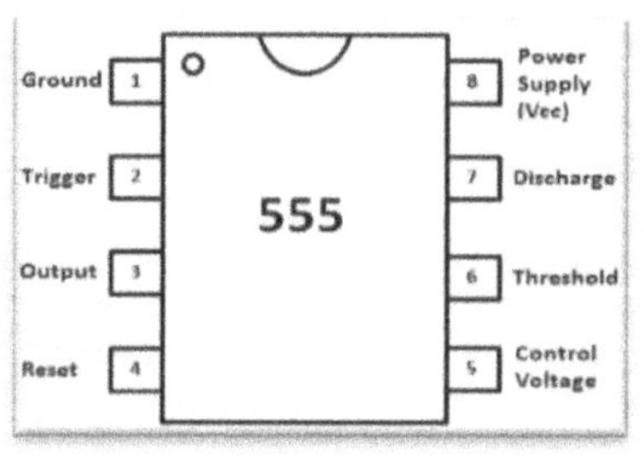

Pin Diagram

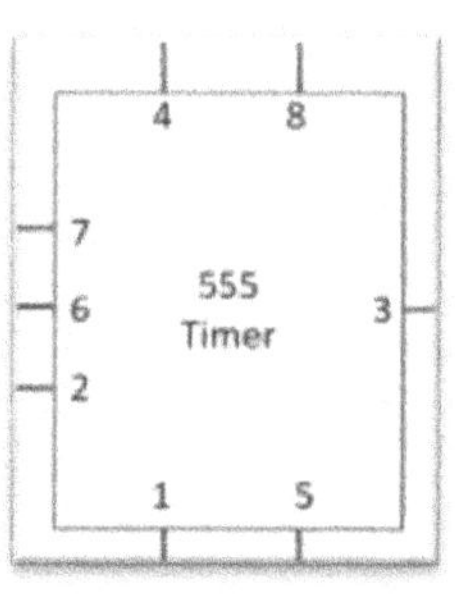

Symbol in Circuits

Identifying the Pins

Look for a notch on the surface of the plastic package. Hold it towards your left as shown in the figure. The left most pin at the bottom layer will be pin 1. Move finger in the anti clock wise direction. Next one to the right of 1 will be pin 2, then pin 3 and then pin 4. Now continue to the upper layer, again in the anti clock direction. The right most pin in the upper layer will be Pin 5. The one to the left 6, next 7 and the left most on the upper layer will be pin 8.

LM 741 Op Amp

741 Op Amp IC is widely used in analog circuits due to its versatility. It can work as a comparator, where it compares two input voltage signals and produces an output based on the input voltages. It is also widely used as oscillators for generating sinusoidal, square and triangular waveforms.

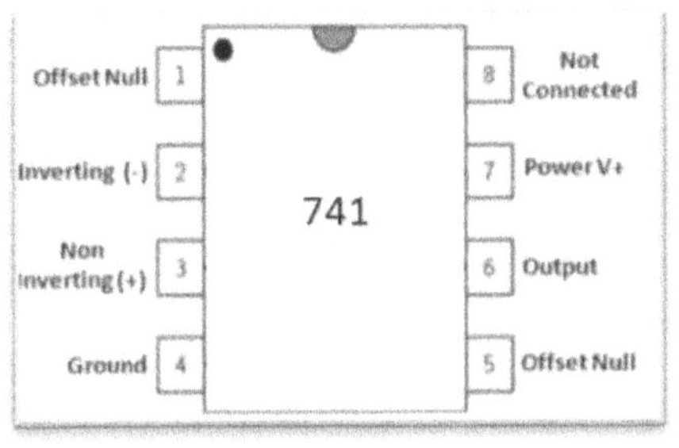

Pin Diagram   **Symbol in Circuits**

Identifying the Pins

Pins of 741 are identified by the same method that was used for IC 555. Hold the IC with the notch towards your left. Left most pin at the bottom is pin 1. Proceed in anti clock direction to identify the remaining pins.

Circuit Diagram

Before delving into the toolkit, let's grasp the concept of a circuit diagram. It's a visual representation, using standard electrical symbols, to depict an electrical circuit. Drawing a simple circuit diagram is actually the first step in electronics, as it helps establish an accurate connection layout for the intended circuit.

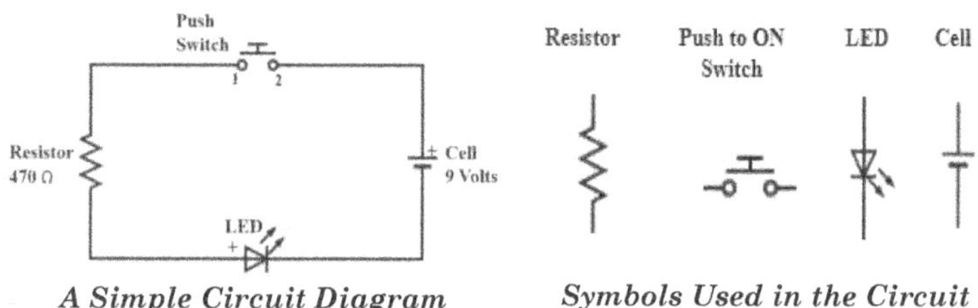

A Simple Circuit Diagram   *Symbols Used in the Circuit*

Each electronic component is represented by a unique symbol in the circuit diagram. The value of the component in standard units will be written alongside. We'll become familiar with these symbols as we discuss each component in detail.

A solid line connecting one component to another signifies a connection between them. When multiple components are connected to the same point or when two components are interconnected, we denote the junction with a solid dot.

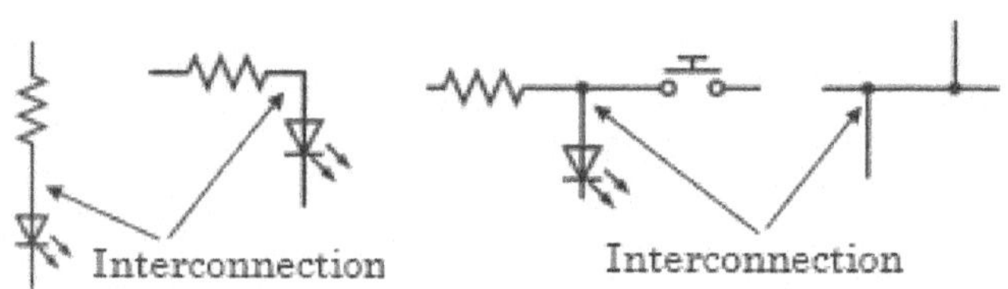

Representing Interconnections in a Circuit Diagram

The interconnections in the circuit diagram shown above can be observed with the actual circuit elements below:

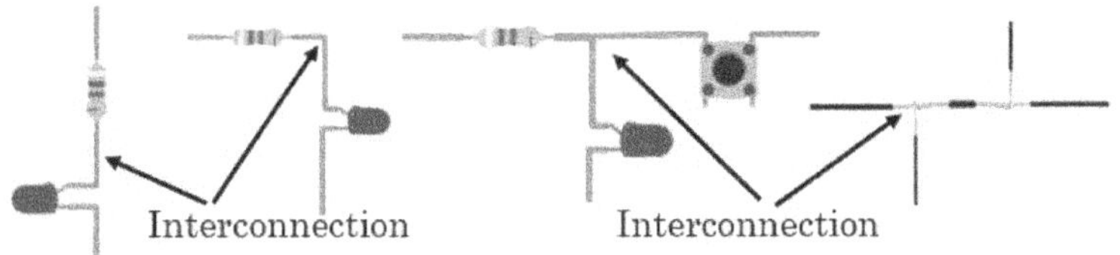

Representing Interconnections in actual Circuit

Two wires crossing without a solid dot at the intersection in a circuit imply no connection, indicating that the wires are simply crossing paths without being connected. Sometimes, the crossover is denoted using a half-circle at the point of crossover.

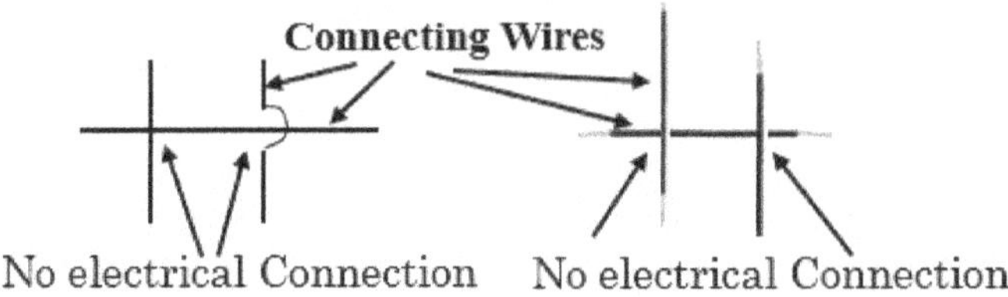

In the next session, we will demonstrate how these interconnections and wire crossings are wired on a breadboard.

Bread Board

Every gadgets have electronic circuits with components mounted on Printed Circuit Boards (PCBs) and soldered firmly. As a beginner, you may find assembling a circuit on a PCB a bit challenging for a few reasons. Firstly, you need to learn how to handle a soldering iron properly – incorrect handling could result in burns on your little fingers! Secondly, once you solder a component, you can't reuse it for other experiments unless you carefully remove the solder and extract the component from the PCB.

That is where a breadboard becomes handy for creating our experimental circuits, allowing us to easily mount and dismount the components. No soldering skills are required to facilitate your learning. Just follow the circuit diagram, place all the components correctly on the board, and interconnect them with wires to make it work!

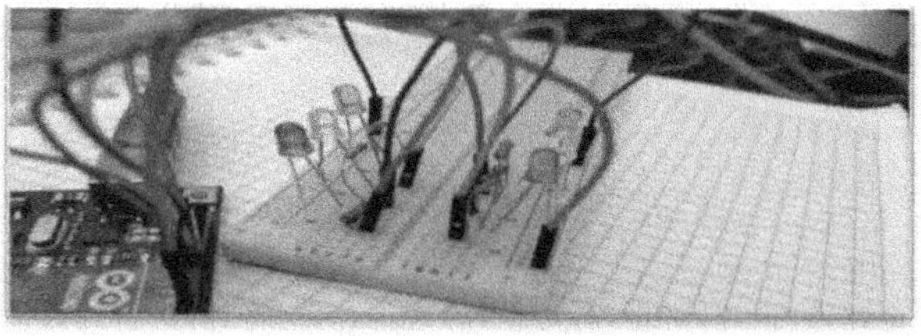

A breadboard is a type of circuit board that is very useful for building and testing prototypes. Beginners can use the breadboard to become familiar with circuits without the need for soldering.

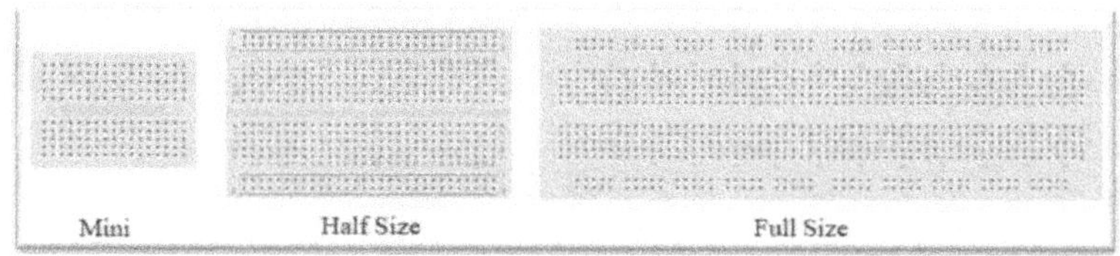

Breadboards come in three sizes: mini, half, and full-size boards, with 170, 400, and 830 points (holes) respectively. For simpler circuits with few components, a mini board will suffice. For larger circuits, a full-size board or even multiple boards may be necessary.

The figure below shows the interconnectivity of points on the breadboard.

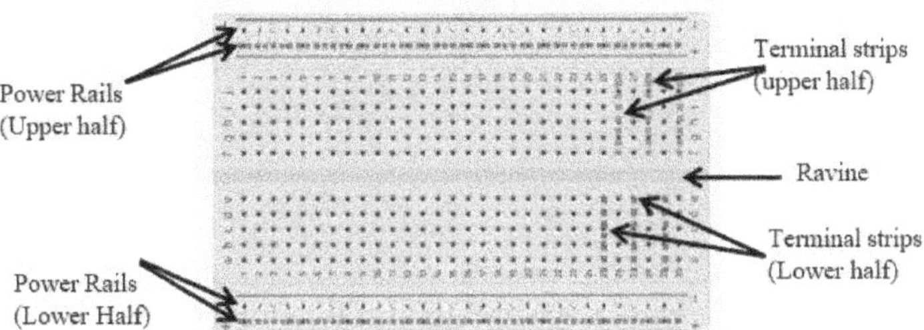

The holes in the breadboard are arranged into rows and columns. There are four horizontal rows at the top and bottom of the breadboard, serving as power rails: one each for positive supply and ground supply at both the top and bottom. All the points on each row are internally interconnected, making it easier to access the power supply for the circuit components.

Please note that the upper and lower power rails mentioned above are not internally connected. It's a better practice to establish the interconnection externally, to enable easy tapping of power from both the top and bottom halves on the board.

Similarly, each of the terminal strips (with five holes each) is interconnected and acts as a single connection point. Please note that the terminal strips on the upper and lower halves, separated by the ravine (a groove between the upper and lower halves), are not interconnected and function as separate points.

The ravine enables placing of switches and dual in-line package Integrated Circuits (such as NE 555 and 741) on the breadboard.

Connecting Leads

Unless we interconnect various terminal strips and also connect the terminal strips to the power rails, the circuit will not be complete. Wires will be necessary for this. You may use simple wires to make the connection, but not all wires work well on the board. The ends of the wires has to be stiff enough to insert in to the hole without bending.

Readily available, Jumper wires are very handy as connectors during circuit assembly on a breadboard. The end points can be easily inserted into the holes to complete the wiring.

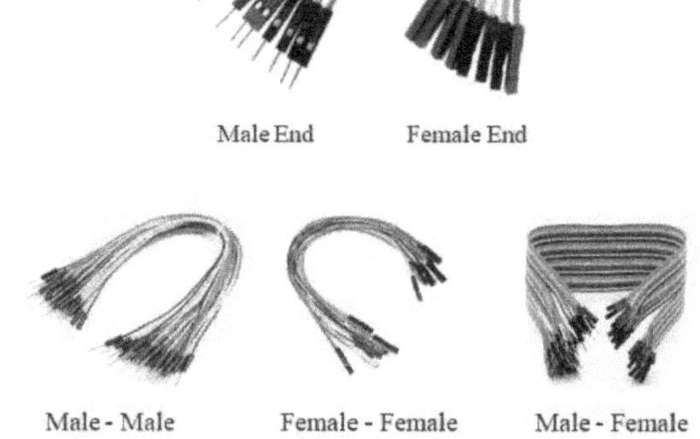

Based on the type of ends, the jumper wires are of three type - 'Male – Male', 'Male-Female' and 'Female-Female'.

On a breadboard, we have to use the 'Male-Male' connector for inter connecting the points. When we need to connect certain components, that can not be fitted on the breadboard due to their construction or size (eg Relays, sensors etc), we may have to use the appropriate type of connectors.

The commercially available jumper wires will be of standard length of 20 cms. In most cases, you will not be needing such long wires as the points will be hardly a few centimeters apart. This would often clutter the board and accessing components behind the clutter of wires on the board would be a real pain.

Instead, if you dare to spend some time, you can make suitable connectors all by yourself.

Get a few meters of 20 SWG wire from the local electronic shop, and cut them into small pieces of suitable lengths. Strip the insulation at both ends for half a centimeter each, with a wire stripper.

Fig: Custom Made Connectors

Ensure that the end points are straight without any bends or protrusions. You could use a nose plier to straighten the end points if necessary. Your hand made connecting leads are ready for use!

Let us now practice fixing the components on the breadboard and interconnecting them.

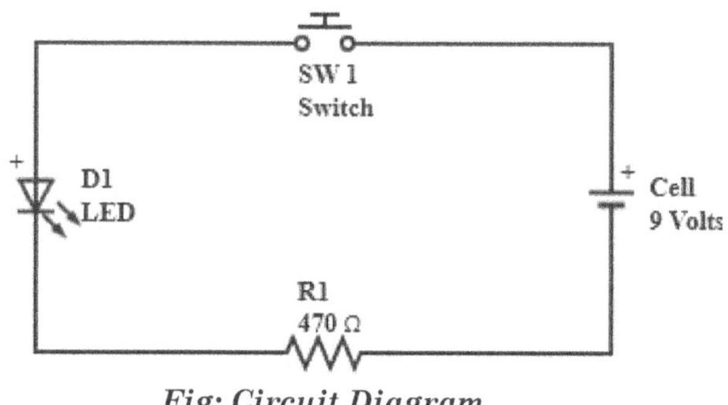

Fig: Circuit Diagram

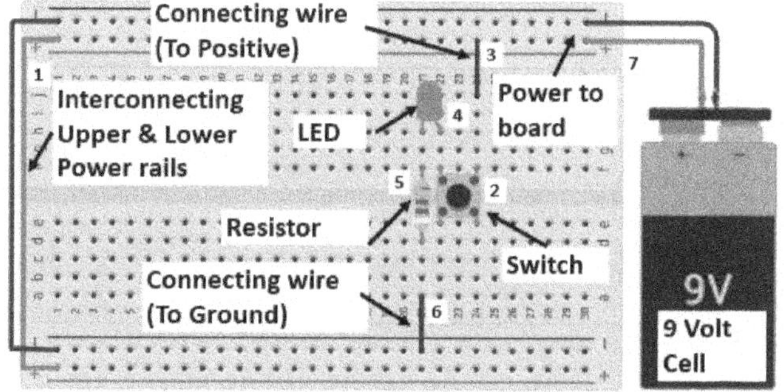

Fig: Layout of Components on Breadboard

Above, you can see a simple circuit diagram and the arrangement of components on the breadboard. This illustration will help you understand how to position components and establish connections on the board. In order to make a bit clearer, I'll guide you through the whole process, step by step.

Step 1: Inter connect the upper and lower power rails using jumper wires. Make sure to link the rail labeled with a + sign at the top to its corresponding counterpart at the bottom. Likewise, connect the one marked with a – sign at the top to the rail marked with a – sign.

Step 2: Place the push switch on the board across the ravine as shown in the figure.

Step 3: Interconnect the terminal strip on which one leg of the switch is connected, to the positive line of the upper power rail.

Step 4: Place the LED on the board, with it's anode on the same terminal strip where the other leg of the switch is connected, and the cathode to the adjacent terminal strip as shown.

Step 5: Inter connect the terminal strip, which is connected with the cathode (- ve) of LED, to the directly opposite terminal strip on the bottom half of the board using the resistor as shown in the figure.

Step 6: Inter connect the terminal strip in the lower half, where the other end of the resistor is connected, to the –ve power rail on the bottom half.

Step 7: Connect the battery clip to the upper (or lower) power rail, in the correct polarity. Positive end (Red wire) should be connected to the positive rail and the negative (Black wire) should be connected to the negative power rail.

After completing all the connections, pressing the push switch would illuminate the LED.

Care Points

When delving into electronics, it's beneficial to adopt good practices right from the start. The breadboard is a delicate device and needs to be handled with care. A few points regarding this are mentioned below:

1. Ensure that the components are neatly arranged on the breadboard, avoiding clutter to facilitate easy fitting and removal during assembly or any necessary changes.

2. Utilize the terminal strips for interconnecting components wherever possible. For example, in the above figure, the positive terminal of the LED is placed on the same terminal strip where one leg of the switch is connected. Alternatively, you can place the LED on any other terminal strip and connect its anode to the terminal strip connected to the switch using a wire. However, this will increase the number of wires on the board.

3. Ensure that the legs of the components are inserted vertically into the holes on the board. Placing them at an angle may cause the thin connectors inside the holes to widen, leading to loose contact and quicker wear.

4. The battery should be connected to the board only after all components are placed on the board, connections are completed, and a quick check is performed vis-à-vis the circuit diagram. Please remove the battery clip from the board before any

changes are made to the wiring. Once the experiment is over, make it a point to remove the battery supply to avoid draining out the battery.

5. If the holes in a terminal strip are insufficient to connect all components or wires, never force multiple wires or components into the same hole as a temporary solution. This can damage the hole. Instead, utilize a free adjacent terminal strip as an extension by interconnecting both terminal strips with a wire.

6. Straighten the terminals of the components before fitting them onto the board to ensure proper contact with the breadboard holes and prevent potential damage to the terminal strip.

7. Do not grab and pull all the components together, while removing them from the breadboard after each experiment. Instead, pull each component and wires one after the other, without twisting or bending. It is a better practice to straighten the legs straightaway to keep it ready for the next experiment.

8. Avoid spilling water or any liquid on the breadboard, as this can cause a short circuit and potentially lead to permanent damage.

9. When not in use, ensure it is covered to prevent dust from entering the holes, which could lead to poor terminal contact.

Few Other Components Included in the Kit

An introduction in to a few more components would be essential before we start our hands on.

Light Dependent Resistor (LDR)

It is a type of resistor, which changes its resistance based on the light that falls on it. The resistance decreases with increase in light intensity and vice versa. This property makes the LDR an integral component, wherever we need to measure the intensity of light.

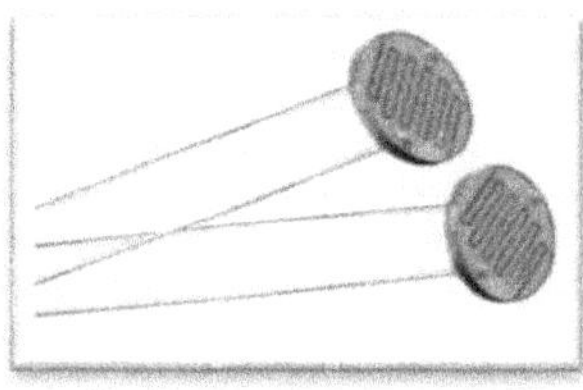

LDR

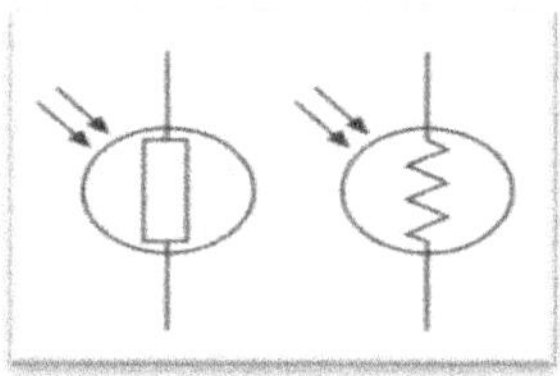

Symbols Used

Just like a resistor, the LDR also has two unmarked legs, and could be connected in the circuit either way, without bothering about the right polarity.

Variable Resistor (Potentiometer)

It is a three terminal resistor, where the electric resistance value at the middle terminal can be varied by turning the attached knob.

Variable Resistor

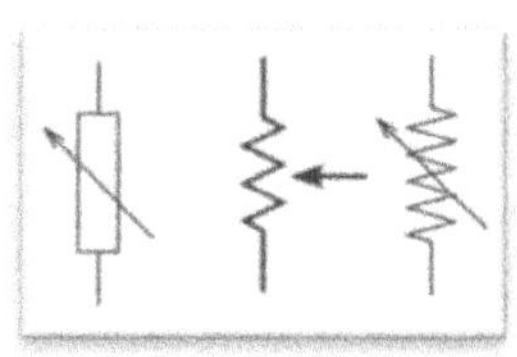

Symbols Used

In circuits, they are useful in setting a predefined value of resistance, which in turn sets a reference voltage at a point in the circuit.

Though the potentiometer comes in various shapes and values, we will be using a preset type that can be conveniently fitted on our breadboard.

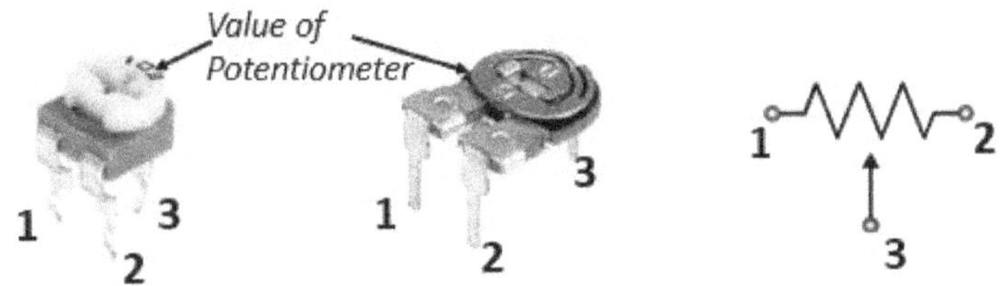

Fig. Finding Value & Identifying Potentiometer Legs

Value of potentiometer will be printed on the slider as shown above, either the direct value, eg- 1M (1 Mega Ohm), 100K (100 Kilo Ohm) or in a coded value eg- 103 (Stands for 10, followed by three 0s, ie 10000 Ohms, or 10Kilo Ohms).

If pin 1 & 2 are used in the circuit, it will include the maximum resistance, and rotating the slider will not introduce any change in resistance.

In order to control the resistance by turning the slider, we should use the pin 3 along with one or both the fixed terminals as shown below.

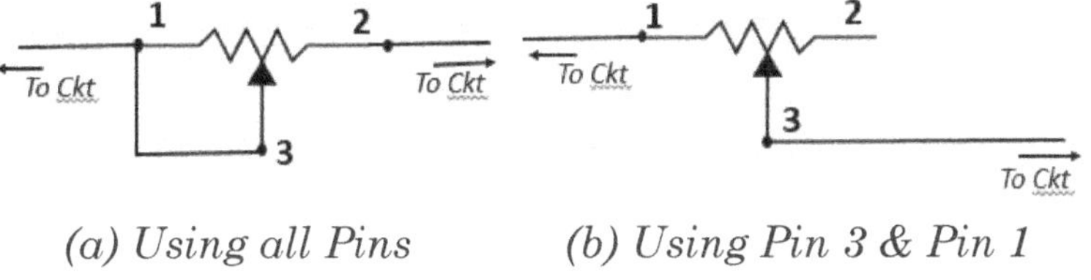

(a) Using all Pins   *(b) Using Pin 3 & Pin 1*

Thermistor

A Thermistor is a type of resistor, whose resistance is controlled by the surrounding temperature. Hence, we can use a thermistor as a sensor to monitor temperature. There are two types, PTC (Positive Temperature Coefficient) - whose resistance increases with the temperature, and NTC (Negative Temperature Coefficient) - whose resistance decreases when the surrounding temperature increases.

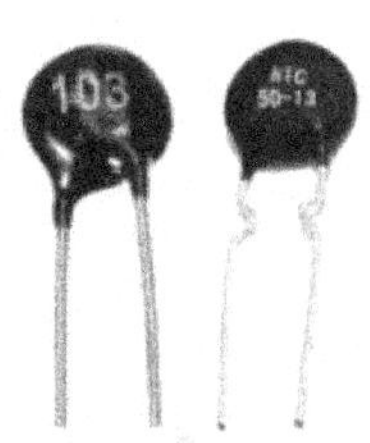

Like a LDR, the thermistors too have two unmarked legs, which permits you to connect it in the circuit in any direction. In the kit, we have included a 4.7K (Labelled 472), NTC-type thermistor.

IR Trans – Receiver Pair

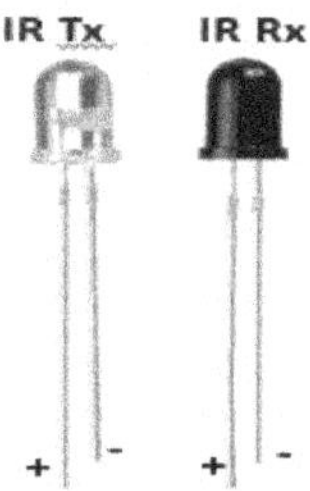

IR Transmitter LED (white colour) continuously emits lights in IR spectrum (not visible to human eye) and the IR Receiver LED (Black colour) receives the reflections from objects in the near vicinity.

Anode and Cathode terminals can be identified by following the method adopted for normal LED.

Caution- IR LEDs do not emit visible lights, hence can not be used to replace standard LEDs.

Avoid pointing IR LEDs towards human eye, as the IR light could be harmful for the eyes.

Buzzer, Loud Speaker, Microphone

A buzzer or beeper is an audio signaling device. Buzzers are used in alarm and signaling devices.

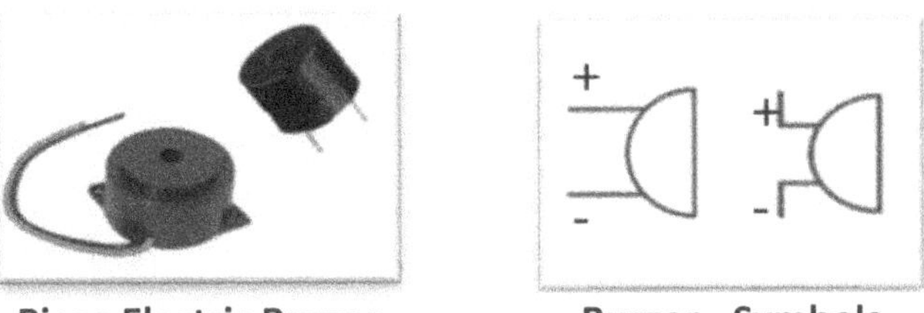

Piezo Electric Buzzer   **Buzzer - Symbols**

A buzzer has positive/negative terminals and needs to be connected in the right polarity in a circuit.

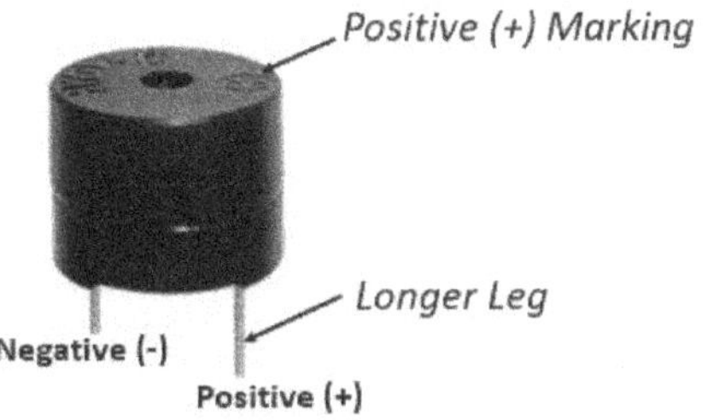

Fig. Identifying terminals of a buzzer

The terminals can be distinguished by two ways:

1. Inspect both the legs closely. The one with a longer leg will be the Positive Terminal and the other will be the negative terminal.

2. Look for a + sign on the top face of the plastic body of the buzzer. Pin directly against that sign will be Positive Terminal.

Speakers are used as audio output device, to reproduce the audio from the output signals of an audio amplifier. It has two terminals, that could be connected in a circuit either way, without being bothered about the polarity.

Speaker

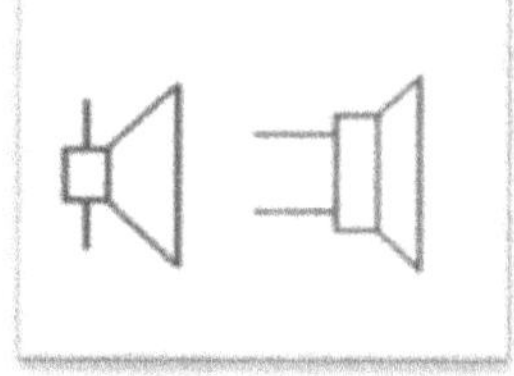

Speaker - Symbols

A microphone is an input device, used to detect sound waves and convert them to electrical signals.

Microphone

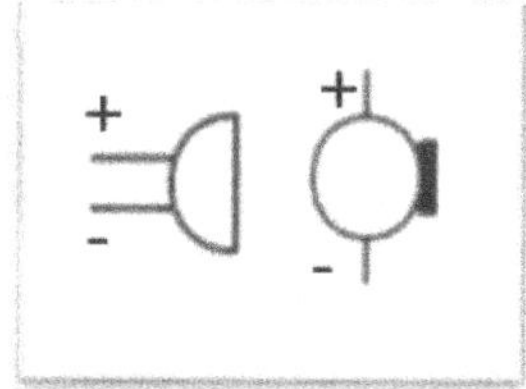

Microphone - Symbols

For the circuits here, we will use a condenser microphone. We need to identify the positive and negative terminals correctly.

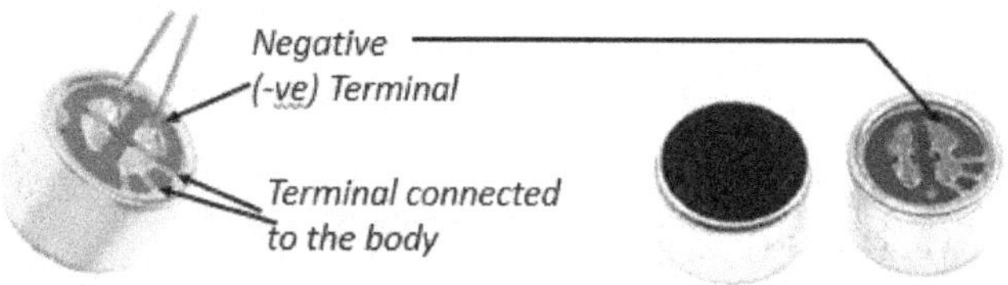

Fig. Identifying terminals of a Microphone

Look at the bottom. Terminal that is connected to the body using thin metallic strips, will be the negative (- ve) terminal.

Often, microphones comes without a lead or wire protruding from the terminal points. In such cases, you need to attach two wires by soldering to the terminal points, to extend it to breadboard.

Switches

A switch is a device used to connect or disconnect electrical power to a circuit. It is also used as input device to interrupt ongoing operation or to activate a specific function in the circuit. There are many types of switches, but for the item being we will be using two types of switches only, ie Toggle switch, and Push Switch.

A toggle switch is used to select between two stable positions (ON and OFF), and it remains in the selected position till it is reverted back. Example is the fan/light switches in our homes.

Toggle Switch

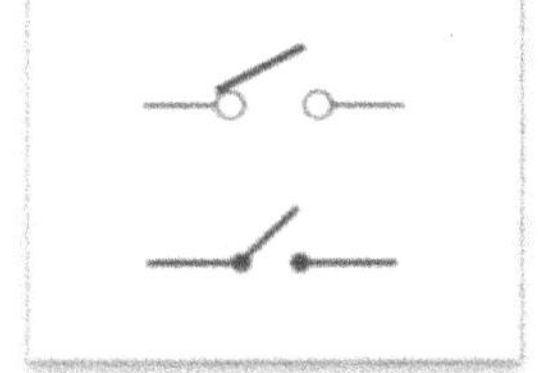

Toggle Switch - Symbols

A push switch is used to temporarily connect or disconnect a part of the circuit for activating a certain function. It can be used as a start/stop or set/reset switch. They are generally used as an input device in circuits.

Push Switch

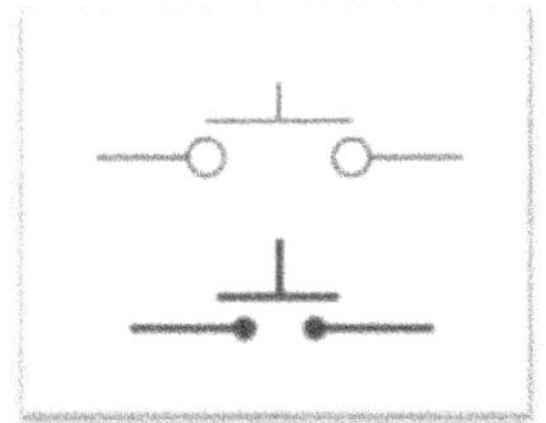

Push Switch - Symbols

In all our experiments, a four-leg push switch is used. On the breadboard, the push switch is to be fixed across the ravine, as shown below.

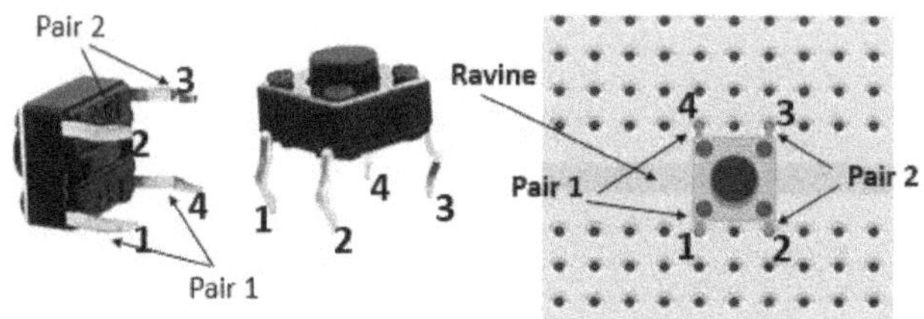

Fig – Fixing the push switch on the breadboard

Identify the two pairs (positioned in opposite sides) of legs 1/4 and 2/3. They are normally connected, even when the switch is not pressed. When the switch is pressed, the adjacent legs (i.e., Legs 1&2, and Legs 3&4 as illustrated) get inter connected. While assembling circuits on the breadboard, you have to use two terminals to complete the wiring. You could use one leg each from the two pairs (i.e. one of the following combinations - Leg 1 / Leg 2 or Leg 3 / Leg 4 or Leg 1 / Leg 3 or Leg 2 / Leg 4). Using any other combination (i.e. Leg 1/Leg 4 or Leg 2/Leg 3), will make the switch non effective!

This will give you the flexibility to use suitable combination, depending on the ease of using the upper or lower half of the board for connection.

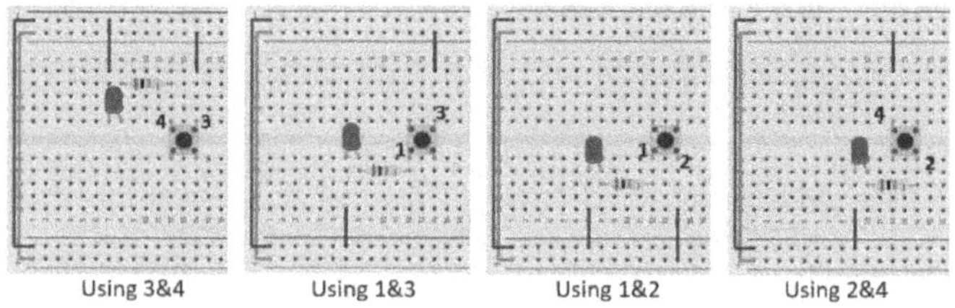

Fig – Different Layout of a switch on the board

Battery (Cell)

Batteries or cells provide dc supply to electronic circuits. They come in different size and capacities.

| 1.5 Volt Cells | 9 Volt Cell | Battery Symbol |

A normal cell (AA or AAA) provides 1.5 volt dc. Most of the electronic circuits are designed work safely on 5 – 9 volts of supply voltage. If you decide to use this battery for powering the circuit, we have to use a battery holder, which can hold four AA batteries, and provide 6 volts as output.

| 2 Battery Holder | 4 Battery Holder | 9 Volt Battery Clip |

We will be using a 9 volt cell for all our experiments. This can be connected easily to the circuit using the battery clip.

The cell has distinct positive and negative terminals, each marked with unique features (the male pin is positive, and the female pin is negative). Attach the battery clip correctly to the cell (Connect the female pin of the clip to the male pin of the cell and vide versa). The positive terminal is identified by the red-colored lead of the battery clip, while the negative terminal will be the black-colored lead.

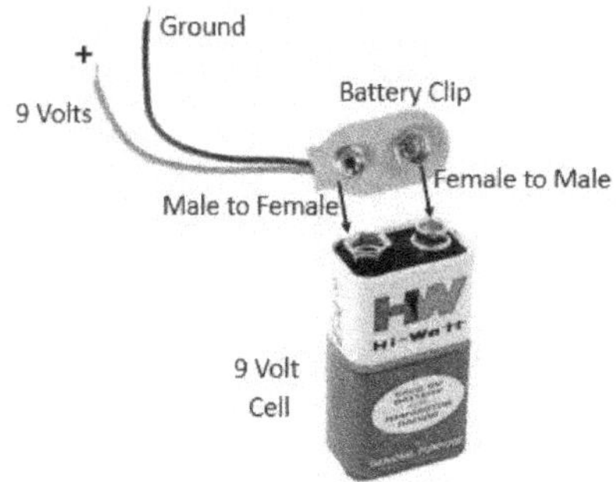

You may have to attach a firm wire at the end of both terminal wires of the battery clip for inserting easily on the breadboard.

Care Points

1. Battery Terminals should never be shorted.

2. Ensure that the battery is connected to the circuit in the correct polarity, to avoid damage to components.

3. Utmost care should be taken while handling and disposing off the used batteries, to prevent contact with hazardous chemicals.

4. Disconnect the battery immediately after the experiment. Keeping it connected to the circuit for long, could result in draining out the charge from the battery.

MAKE YOUR OWN SENSORS!

Imagine a world where everyday objects come alive, perceiving their surroundings and responding in real-time. Sensors are the unsung heroes of this world, tirelessly monitoring conditions and prompting actions when needed.

In this chapter, we'll embark on a journey into the heart of sensor creation. From the familiar territory of light and temperature sensors to the uncharted waters of touch, moisture, rain, and water level sensors, we'll explore the art of crafting these ingenious devices from scratch.

Touch Sensors

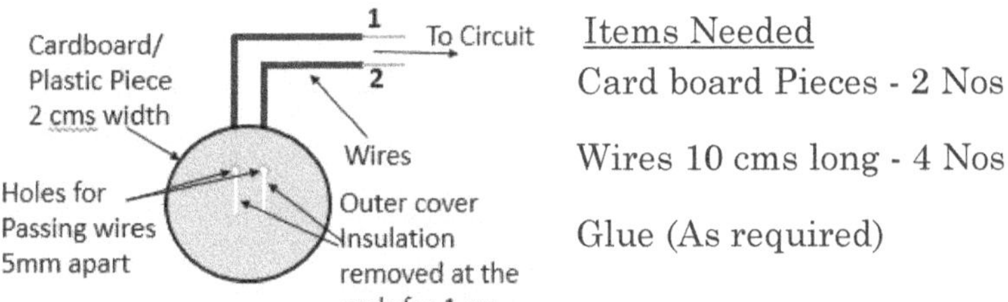

Take a piece of cardboard or plastic, about 2 centimeters wide. Make two holes at the middle of it, spaced half a centimeter apart, as shown. Strip the PVC sheathing from both ends of the wires, exposing about 1 centimeter of bare wire. Bring one end of each wire to the top face of the cardboard through the holes, ensuring they do not touch.

Bend the wires and firmly affix them to the cardboard using glue, being careful not to spread glue onto the top of exposed wire ends, as this could hinder contact when touched. The other ends of the wires, labeled as point 1 and 2, can be extended to the circuit.

We will be needing two such sensors: one for powering on and the other for powering off.

Moisture Sensor Probes

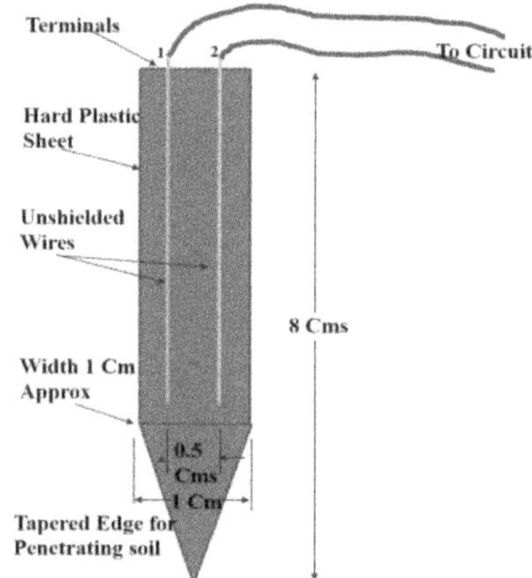

Cut the sheet into the shape as illustrated. Take two wires, about 10 cm long and strip off the insulating shield for half of their length. Firmly attach the unshielded wires to the plastic sheet using glue as shown, taking care not to spread the glue over the top face of the naked wire. Ensure there is a safe gap of 5 mm between the wires to prevent electrical contact. Free ends of the wires, labeled as 1 and 2, can be extended to our circuit.

The moisture sensor probe is now ready and can be inserted into the soil in the flower pot.

Water Level sensor (For Water Tank Model)

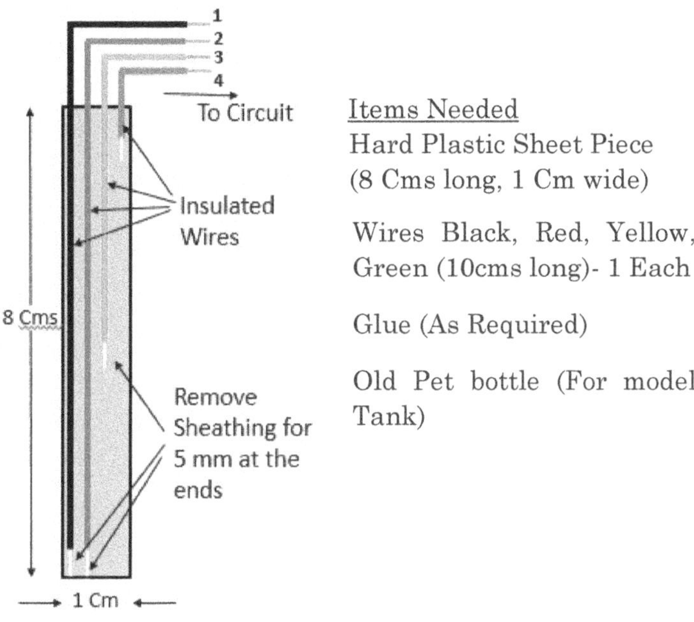

Cut the sheet into the shape as illustrated. Take four wires: Black and Red wires, each 10 cm long; Yellow and Green wires, approximately 6 cm and 4 cm long, respectively. Strip off the insulating shield for about 5 millimeters at both ends of the wires.

Secure the wires on the sheet as shown, using glue. Position the red wire and the common wire (black) tip at the bottom of the tank. Ensure there is a safe gap of 2 mm between the open ends to prevent electrical contact. Similarly, place the yellow wire and green wire tips at the half-water level mark and full level, respectively. Our Water level sensor is ready for use!

We can create a water tank model using a plastic bottle cut to approximately 8 cm in height. Secure the sensor that we just made inside the model tank using double-sided tape. Extend the other ends of the wires, labeled as 1, 2, 3, and 4, to the circuit.

Rain Sensor Probes

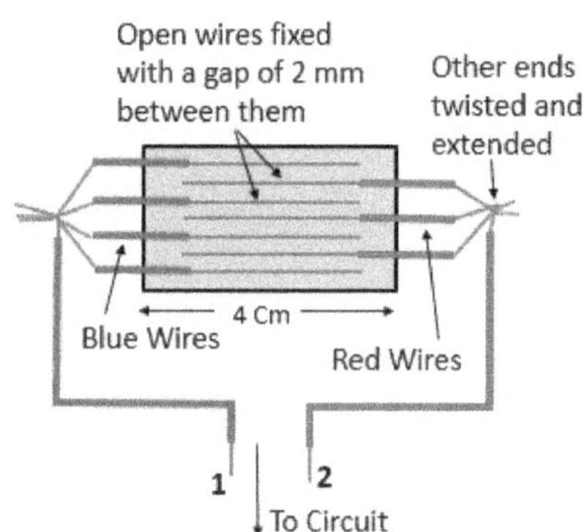

<u>Items Needed</u>
Hard Plastic Sheet Piece (4 cm X 2 cm)

Wires 6 cm long, Red and blue colour five pieces each

Glue (As Required)

Remove the sheathing for about 3 cm at one end of the wires. Secure the red and blue wires from both sides on the sheet as illustrated. Maintain a gap of about 2 mm between the exposed wires on the board. Use glue to carefully fix the wires onto the sheet. Ensure that the glue doesn't spill over and playing as an insulating coating on the wires.

Fix all the wire pieces as shown. Twist the free ends of the blue and red wires separately and then extend using two wires to points 1 and 2. This can be further extended to the circuit.

Note - Sensors we created are strictly for our experiment propose only and not suitable for real use circuit implementation.

IT IS TIME FOR THE ACTION

By now, you have a fair idea of the components we'll be working with. It's time to put them all together and create some fascinating circuits that will delight both your eyes and ears!

We'll begin with a simple LED flashlight, a project I mentioned earlier. This will be followed by several circuits using transistors, showcasing their versatility and functionality. We'll also build a few simple circuits with real practical applications, demonstrating how these components come together in everyday electronics.

Next, we'll dive into working with two essential integrated circuit chips: the NE 555 timer IC and the LM 741 Op Amp IC. These powerful chips will open up a new realm of possibilities, allowing us to design more complex and interesting circuits.

You may find it a bit confusing at the beginning, but once you get the hang of it, it will become a piece of cake. Identifying the right component and distinguishing the correct pins is crucial in circuit implementation. I have included a resistance color code chart at the end of this book for all the resistors that I have used, which may assist you in choosing the right one. Some of these concepts, such as pin identification, have already been explained in the component section. Specific details, if any, will be introduced as we discuss each circuit in detail.

To help you along the way, each session includes a pictorial image of the setup, providing clarity on the placement of components on the breadboard. These visual aids are designed to make the learning process smoother and more intuitive. However, I advise you not to solely rely on the pictorial images. It's important to understand the concepts of circuit diagrams and gradually learn to place the components on the board without any such assistance.

I have created videos of circuit construction and testing and posted them on my YouTube channel. I recommend watching these videos for a better understanding. They offer step-by-step demonstrations and additional tips that can enhance your learning experience.

Before we commence, please read the 'Care Points' and 'Notes' mentioned with the components again to avoid any damage.

Now, it's time to take our first plunge into the deep ocean of electronic circuits. Get ready to explore, experiment, and enjoy the world of electronics as we build our knowledge one circuit at a time!

LED FLASH LIGHT

Let's begin our adventure by creating a basic circuit using some cool stuff: a tiny LED, a 9-volt battery, a switch, and a resistor. Making a LED circuit is like starting with the ABCs of electronics. This project is perfect for the beginners – it's like building a little electronic friend that's simple and fun to make!

Circuit Diagram

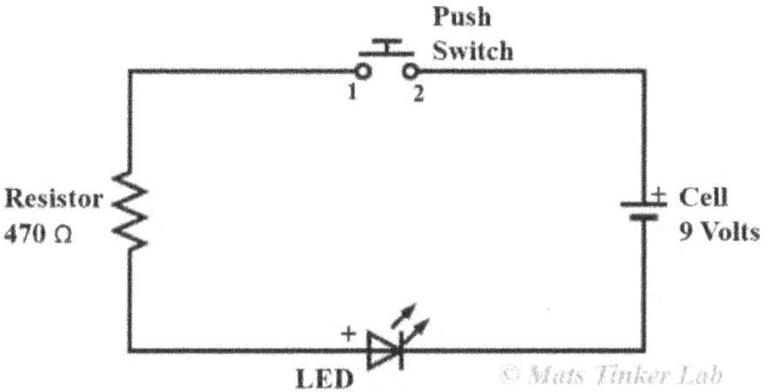

Components List

LED   *– 1 No*   *Push Switch*   *– 1 No*
Resistor 470 Ω   *– 1 No*

This circuit comprises four components: an LED connected in series with a current-limiting resistor, and a switch connected to the battery. When the switch is pressed, current flows, and the LED lights up. The 470 Ω resistor limits the current through the LED to a safe range of 10 to 20 milli amperes.

Follow the circuit diagram and place components on the breadboard one by one. Ensure that the terminals are positioned correctly. Please, refer the component's description, if you are in doubt.

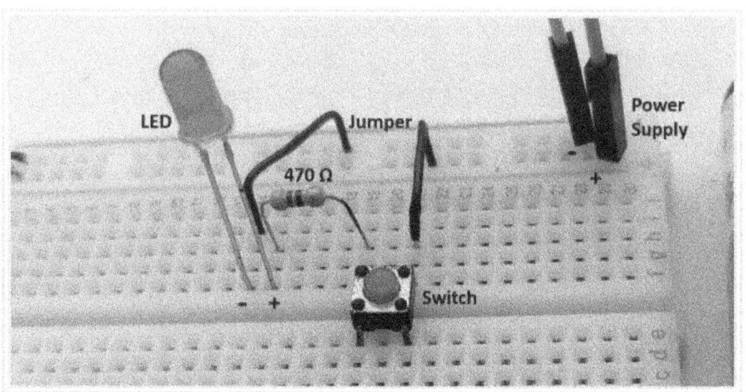

Fig. Simple component Layout on the breadboard

Wherever possible, utilize the terminal strips on the breadboard to interconnect the components. Use connecting leads to link the remaining points.

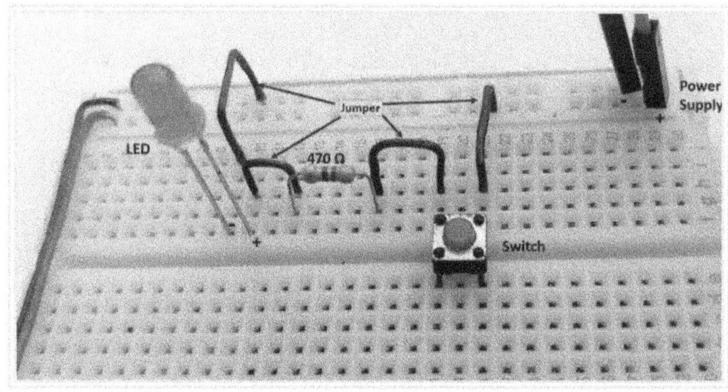

Fig. A distributed component layout approach

A distributed arrangement of components is perfectly fine. But, it may require more number of connecting leads and occupy more terminal strips on the board. Number of components that can be accommodated on the board will be lesser, as the available free terminal strips will be far fewer. In effect, this might pause a limitation while assembling circuits with more components.

<u>TRANSISTOR SWITCH</u>

Let's now delve into how a transistor operates with a straightforward circuit. In this setup, we'll utilize the transistor as a switch to control the connection of an external load, such as an LED.

Circuit Diagram

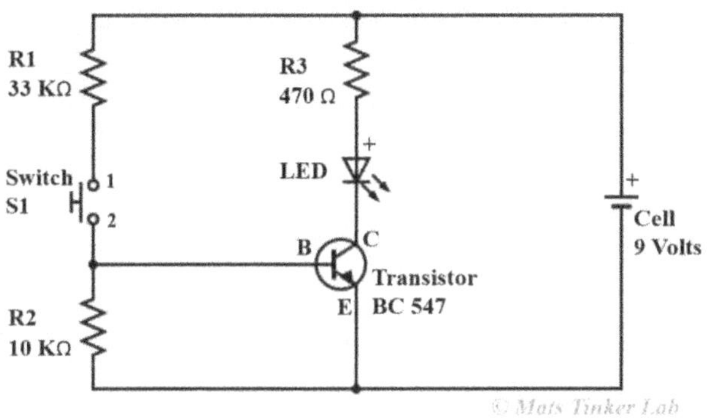

Components List

LED	*– 1 No*	*Push Switch*	*– 1 No*
Transistor BC 547	*– 1 No*	*Resistor 470 Ω*	*– 1 No*
Resistors 10 K, 33 K	*– 1 Each*		

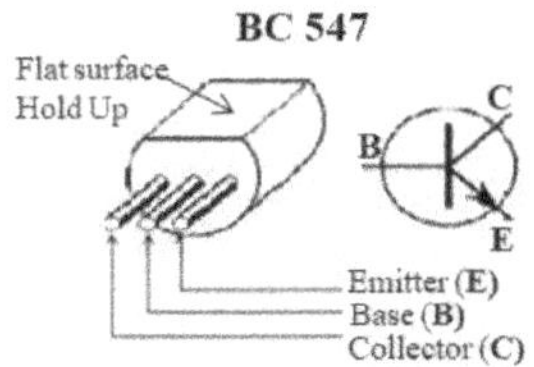

Fig. Identifying the Terminals of a Transistor

BC547 is indeed an NPN transistor. Properly connecting the Base, Collector, and Emitter terminals is crucial for the transistor to function correctly. When holding it with the flat portion facing upwards, the collector terminal will be on the extreme left, the middle one will be the base, and the terminal on the right will be the emitter.

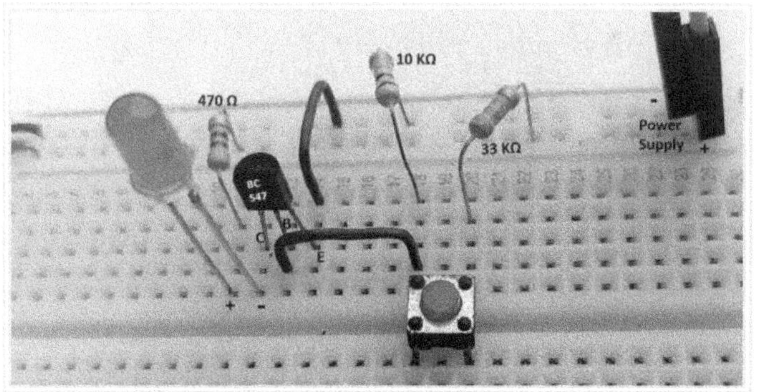

Fig. Component Layout on the breadboard

When the switch is off, the base of the NPN transistor is at a negative potential, which maintains the transistor in the off state. In this state, no current flows through the collector-emitter junction, keeping the LED turned off. However, when the switch is closed, a positive voltage is applied to the base terminal of the transistor, causing it to enter the conduction stage. Consequently, current flows through the Collector-Emitter junction, illuminating the LED.

You might wonder why we use a transistor to activate an LED instead of a simple switch. The primary goal here is to introduce you to the functionality of a transistor. Additionally, you'll discover that employing similar transistor circuits becomes essential in numerous practical situations, as described in the subsequent chapters.

SIMPLE TIMER CIRCUIT

Let's explore the world of timer circuits—smart devices that regulate when things turn on or off, but with a slight time delay. In this fundamental circuit, a small component called a capacitor plays a crucial role. Join us as we uncover the simplicity behind this essential electronic technique.

Circuit Diagram

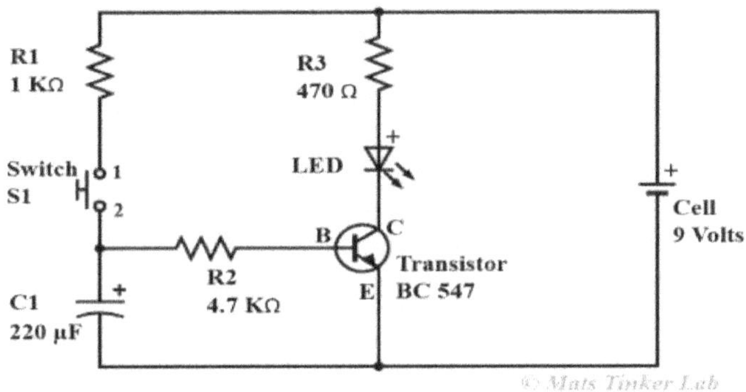

Components List

LED   *– 1 No*   *Push Switch*   *– 1 No*
Transistor BC 547   *– 1 No*   *Capacitor 220 µF*   *– 1 No*
Resistors 470 Ω, 1 KΩ, 4.7 KΩ – 1 Each

A capacitor functions somewhat like a tiny battery. It can be charged by applying a voltage across its terminals. Once the charging voltage is removed, the capacitor retains the charge until a discharge path becomes available. When such a path is available, it discharges the charge.

When switch S1 is pressed, capacitor C1 becomes fully charged through resistor R1. This positive voltage is then applied to the base of the transistor via resistor R2, causing it to enter conduction, which further lights up the LED.

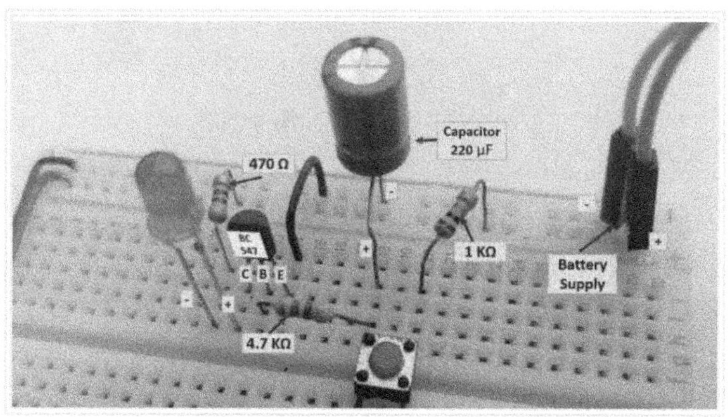

Fig. Component Layout on the breadboard

After releasing the switch, the voltage stored across the capacitor gradually discharges through resistor R2 and the Base-Emitter junction of the transistor. The duration of this discharge is determined by the values of capacitor C1 and discharge resistor R2. After the specified delay, the capacitor completes its discharge, reducing the voltage across it to zero. Consequently, the base voltage of the transistor also drops to zero, causing the transistor to turn off, which shuts off the LED.

RAIN ALARM

A rain alarm is a device crafted to detect the presence of rain or water and activate an alarm. Here, we'll construct a simple circuit capable of sensing rain and triggering a buzzer or LED.

Circuit Diagram

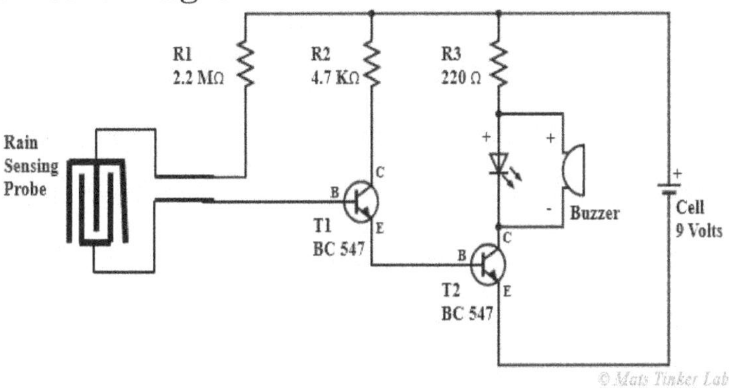

Components List

LED	*– 1 No*	*Buzzer 9 Volts*	*– 1 No*
Transistor BC 547	*– 2 Nos*	*Rain Sensing Probe*	*– 1 No*
Resistors 4.7 K, 2 MΩ	*– 1 Each*	*Resistors 220 Ω*	*– 1 No*

The circuit utilizes two NPN transistors, where the first transistor is used as a driver to switch the second transistor on and off. The rain sensor probe is connected to the base terminal of transistor T1. When there's no rain, the positive voltage through 2.2 MΩ resistor is hanging at the probe terminal. Therefore, T1 remains Off, that keeps T2 in the Off state as well. Consequently, the LED remains Off and the buzzer stays silent.

When raindrops hit the sensor, the resistance between the sensor contacts decreases significantly (due to rainwater's conductivity), leading to a positive voltage being applied to the base of Transistor T1. T1 enters into conduction state, subsequently triggering T2. The LED and the buzzer connected at the output pin (collector) of T2, gets triggered.

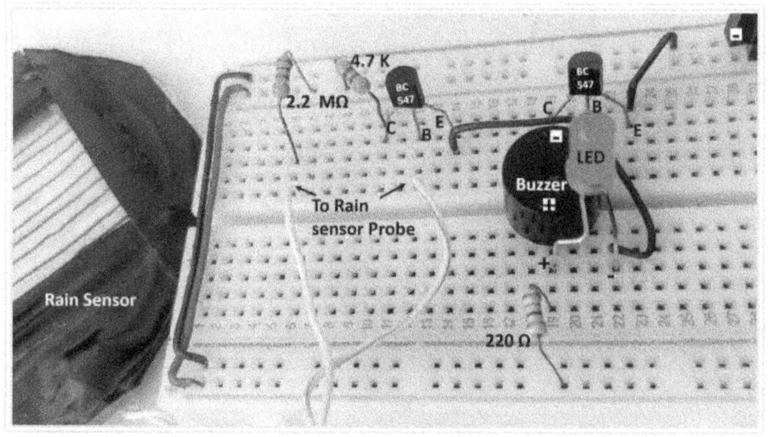

Fig – Component Layout on the breadboard

You can simulate rain by gently pouring a few drops of water onto the sensor. The alarm will remain active as long as the water drops persist on the sensor. To deactivate the alarm, you must thoroughly wipe off all water particles from the sensor contacts.

Be careful not to spill water drops onto the breadboard or components to avoid potential short circuits and damage to the board and components.

AUTO NIGHT LAMP

You might have seen streetlights that light up automatically when it gets dark. This circuit operates on the same principle, automatically triggering the LED when the ambient light falls below a certain level.

Circuit Diagram

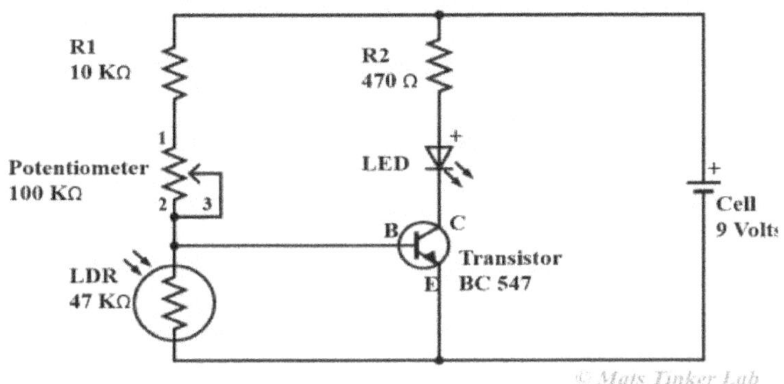

Components List

LED   *– 1 No*   *Transistor BC 547*   *– 1 No*
Resistors 470 Ω, 10 K Ω – 1 Each   *LDR 47 KΩ*   *– 1 No*
Variable Resistor 100 K – 1 No

The LDR serves as a light-sensing device. The resistance of the LDR is inversely proportional to the intensity of light. In simpler terms, as the intensity of light decreases, the resistance increases, and conversely, as the intensity of light increases, the resistance decreases.

The transistor is biased to cutoff, using resistor R1, a potentiometer, and the LDR. Hence, the LED remains off. When the light intensity decreases (such as during dusk), the resistance value of the LDR increases. Consequently, the bias voltage at the base terminal of the transistor becomes more positive, triggering the transistor to On state and causing the LED to illuminate.

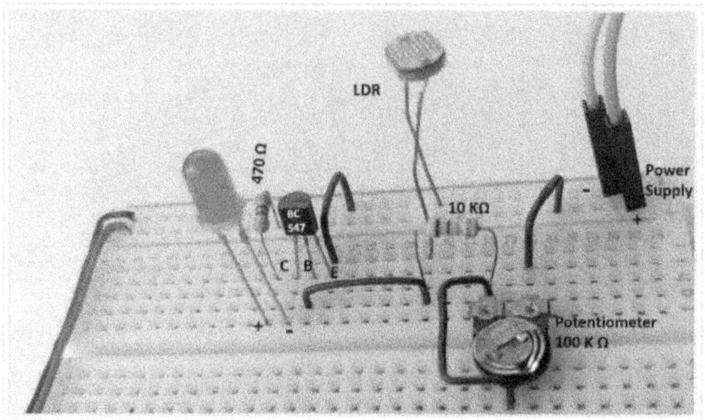

Fig – Component Layout on the breadboard

When the light intensity decreases (for example, during dawn), the resistance of the LDR decreases, leading to a more negative bias voltage at the base terminal. This causes the transistor to go to the cutoff state, switching off the LED.

We can adjust the light intensity at which the transistor turns on/off, by manipulating the potentiometer. When we decrease the resistance (by turning the potentiometer counterclockwise), the bias voltage increases, causing the transistor to activate at a lower intensity of light. Conversely, turning the potentiometer clockwise will make the transistor activate at a higher intensity of light.

TEMPERATURE ALARM

Monitoring the temperature at environments, such as the temperature inside a cold storage unit or an electric grill, is often necessary. Systems are typically implemented to control the temperature with alarms that caution if the temperature exceeds or falls below a certain limit.

Circuit Diagram

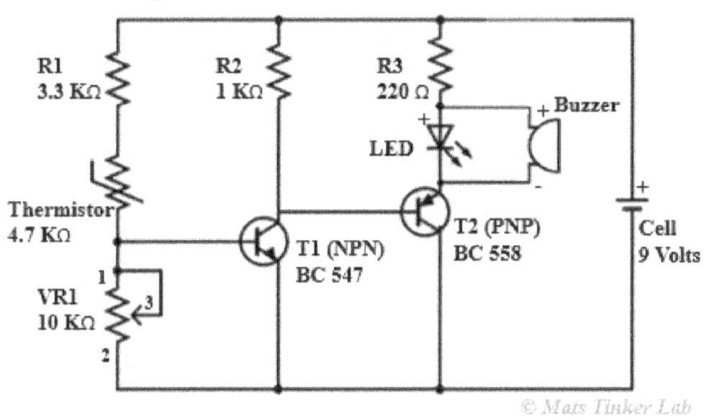

Components List

LED	*– 1 No*	*Buzzer 9 Volt*	*– 1 No*
Transistor BC 547	*– 1 No*	*Transistor BC 558*	*– 1 No*
Variable Resistor 10 K Ω	*– 1 No*	*Thermistor NTC 472*	*– 1 No*
Resistors 220 Ω, 1 K Ω, 4.7 K Ω	*– 1 Ea*		

Variations in the surrounding temperature are measured by temperature sensors. A thermistor is such a sensor, whose resistance varies with changes in the temperature. A PTC type thermistor exhibits a positive temperature coefficient, meaning its resistance increases with rising temperature and decreases with falling temperature. Conversely, the resistance of an NTC type thermistor decreases with rising temperature and increases with falling temperature. For our experiment, an NTC-type thermistor will be used.

The NPN and PNP transistors are connected in a compound pair configuration to achieve maximum gain. Under normal conditions, T1 remains in a cutoff state, ensuring T2 to remain in cutoff. You can increase the temperature by placing a lit matchstick or gas lighter flame near the thermistor. As the temperature increases, the resistance of the thermistor gradually decreases. At a certain temperature, the resistance drops to a level that ensures a positive potential at the base terminal. This turns on transistor T1, subsequently triggering T2. The LED and buzzer activate, indicating that the temperature has exceeded.

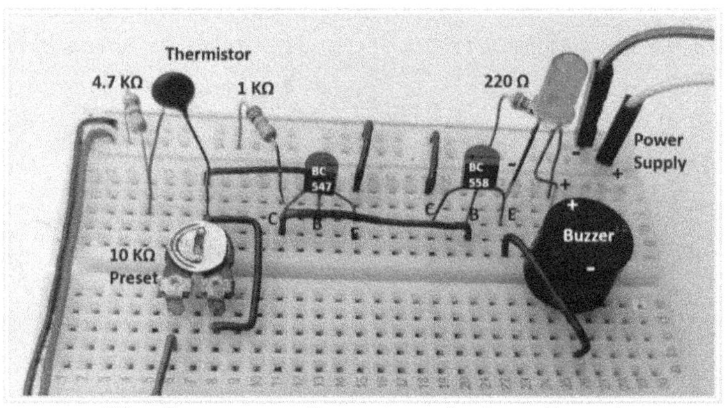

Fig. Component Layout on the breadboard

Variable resistor VR1 can be used to adjust the temperature at which the alarm should get triggered.

LED FLASHER

Flashing lights have long been a source of fascination and creativity in our lives, often adorning our homes during festive occasions. Now, we will delve into the realm of electronics to explore the construction of a simple yet engaging circuit. Our goal is to create a captivating display with two LEDs that flash alternately.

Circuit Diagram

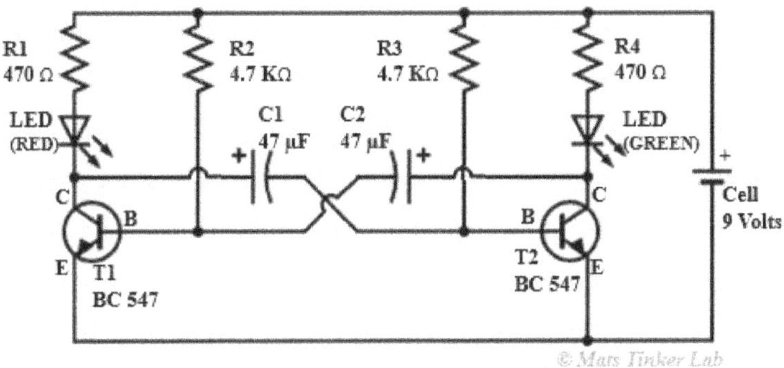

Components List

LED (Green / Red)	*– 1 Each*	*Transistor BC 547*	*– 2 Nos*
Resistor 470 Ω	*– 2 Nos*	*Resistor 4.7 KΩ*	*– 2 Nos*
Capacitor 47 µF	*– 2 Nos*		

There are two NPN transistors, each connected with a LED at the collector pin through a resistor to the positive line. The LED illuminates when the corresponding transistor is powered on. This type of circuit is commonly referred to as an Astable Multivibrator, characterized by its absence of a stable output. Instead, the two transistors switch on and off alternately, producing a high and low output alternately.

Let us assume that T1 is conducting and T2 is in cutoff initially. Charge will build up in C1 through the closed path R3 and CE junction of T1. Once the potential across C1 becomes sufficient enough to trigger T2 (connected to the base of T2), T2 comes on. The voltage at the collector drops to zero (grounded through closed CE junction). This drop is fed to the base of T1 through C2 to power it off.

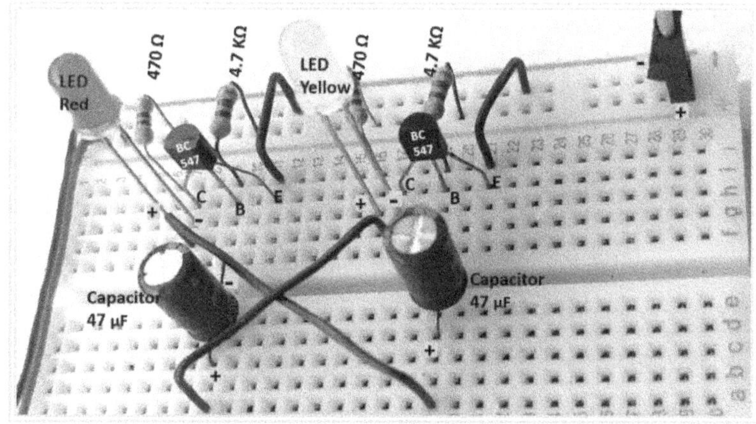

Fig. Component Layout on the breadboard

Now the C2 charges through R2 and CE junction of T2. When the voltage across the C2 becomes sufficient enough to power on T1, T1 comes on. The sudden drop in voltage at the collector pin is fed to the base, through C1 and T2 is turned off. The process repeats and the two transistors turn on and off, effecting the two LEDs to blink alternately.

PROXIMITY SENSOR

A proximity sensor is employed to detect the presence of an object within a specified distance from the sensor. An obstacle-avoiding robot is equipped with this type of sensor to detect when it approaches a close proximity to an object or wall. Now, we would try our hands on a circuit utilizing an IR Transmitter – Receiver pair.

Circuit Diagram

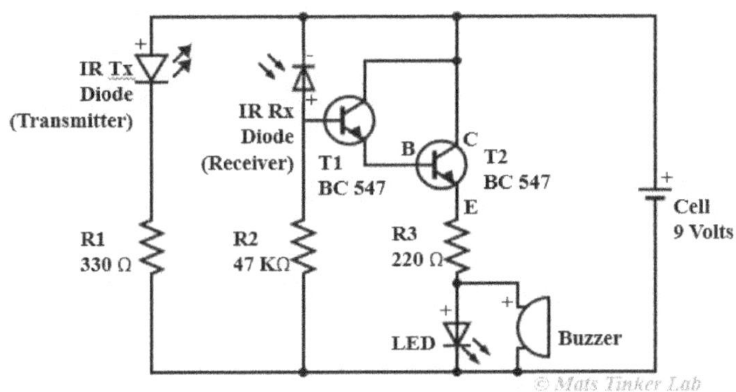

Components List

LED	*– 1 No*	*Buzzer 9 Volt*	*– 1 No*
Transistor BC 547	*– 2 Nos*	*Resistor 220 Ω*	*– 1 No*
Resistors 330 Ω, 47 K	*– 1 Ea*	*IR Tx – Rx Pair*	*– 1 No*

Here the IR Tx – Rx pair are to be arranged side by side, both facing the direction from which the obstruction is to be detected.

When powered on, the IR transmitter continuously emits infrared (IR) light in the forward direction. If any of the light reflects back from objects in close vicinity, the IR receiver detects it. This detection causes the IR receiver to conduct, providing a positive bias voltage at the base of transistor T1.

Here, we have utilized two NPN transistors wired together as a pair, commonly known as a Darlington pair. This configuration provides a significant output current for a minimal input current.

Fig – Component Layout on the breadboard

When the output of the IR receiver is applied to the base, both T1 and T2 are activated. The LED and buzzer, connected to the output terminal, are triggered on, indicating that the IR Tx-Rx pair is in close proximity to an object.

Once the obstruction is removed, the transistors return to the off state, and the light and alarm indications are deactivated.

PLANT WATERING ALARM

A plant watering alarm is a device designed to monitor the moisture level of the soil in a plant pot and provide an alert when the soil becomes too dry. The purpose of such an alarm is to help prevent under-watering of plants, especially in indoor environments where regular monitoring is difficult.

Circuit Diagram

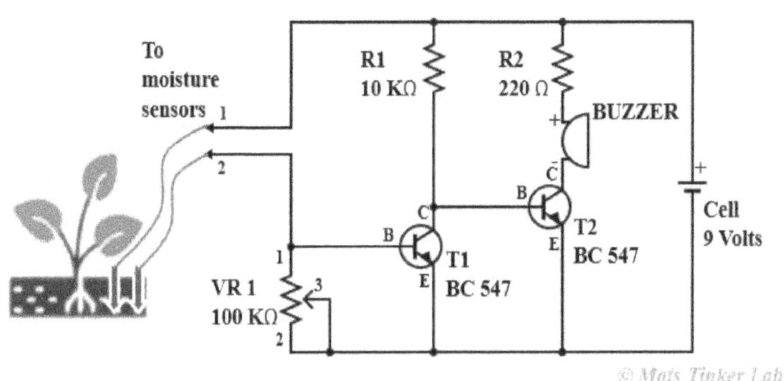

Components List

LED	*– 1 No*	*Buzzer 9 Volt*	*– 1 No*
Transistor BC 547	*– 2 Nos*	*Potentiometer 100 K*	*– 1 No*
Moisture Sensor Probe	*– 1 No*	*Resistors 470 Ω, 10K*	*– 1 Each*

Insert the moisture sensor probe into the soil in the flower pot and connect the probe terminals as shown in the diagram. It is recommended to use a pot with freshly filled or dry soil to test the alarm for the first time.

The circuit utilizes two NPN transistors. Moisture sensor input is connected to the base terminal of T1. If T1 is on, the base voltage of T2 is at zero potential (through C-E junction of T1), which ensures T2 remain off. On the other hand, if T1 is off, the base of T2 get a positive voltage through resistor R1, and triggers it on.

If the soil is dry, T1 remains off, therefore, T2 gets triggered and the alarm comes on, indicating the moisture level in the flower pot is low.

Pour water slowly into the pot. When the moisture level reaches a certain level, the base of T1 gets a positive potential that triggers T1. As a follow up, T2 goes off, deactivating the alarm. The trigger point, which depends on the moisture level in the pot can be adjusted, with the potentiometer VR1.

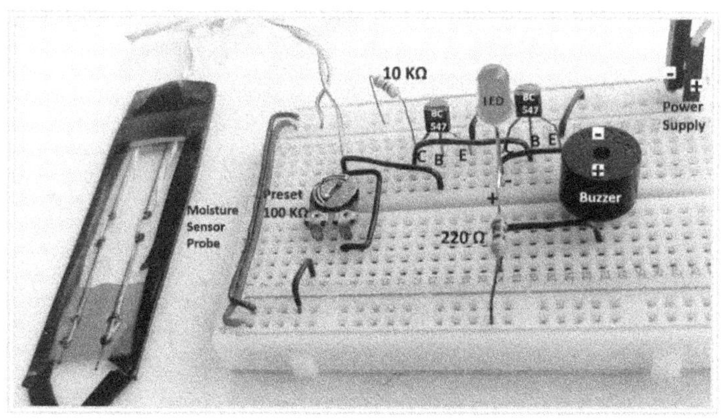

Fig – Component Layout on the breadboard

The circuit will keep monitoring the moisture level in the soil without the need of any human intervention. Whenever the level drops below the set limit, the alarm will get triggered, to remind us for watering the plant.

WATER LEVEL INDICATOR

At home, we all rely on running water from an overhead tank. Many have encountered situations where the tap runs dry. Physically monitoring the water level in the tank isn't always practical. Here, we present a simple circuit to enable remote monitoring of the water level in the tank.

Circuit Diagram

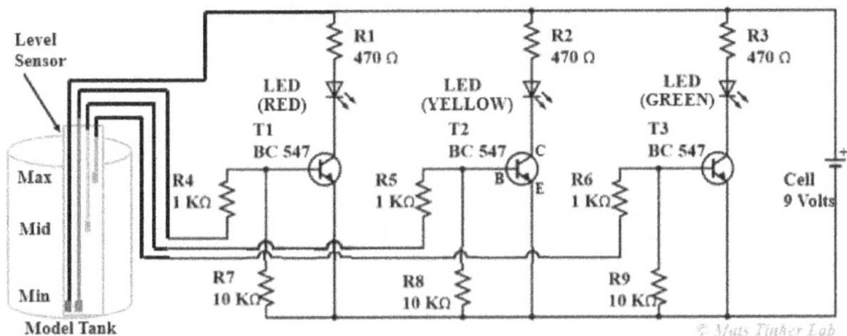

Components List

LED (Red / Yellow / Green) – 1 Ea	*Buzzer 9 Volt*	*– 1 No*
Resistors 1 KΩ, 10 KΩ	*– 3 Ea*	*Resistors 470 Ω*	*– 3 Nos*
Level Sensor Probe	*– 1 No*	*Transistor BC 547*	*– 3 Nos*

The circuit employs three NPN transistors, each connected to a LED at the collector pin. The base of the transistor is connected through a resistor to the corresponding water level sensor terminal. After wiring all components on the board, connect the level sensor and insert it in the model water tank.

Ensure the tank is empty when powering on the circuit. Initially, all LEDs will remain off, indicating there is no water in the tank.

Pour water slowly into the tank. When the water level reaches the bottom mark (red), the positive voltage through the common terminal (black) will reach at the base of the corresponding transistor and trigger it to conduction. As a result the Red LED will light up. As soon as the water level reaches the halfway mark, the yellow light will illuminate in a similar way. Once the tank is full, the green light will also come on.

When the water level in the tank is full, all three LEDs will remain ON. Ideally, only the LED corresponding to the current water level (Green for Full, Yellow for Half & Red for Empty) should have remained ON. It would require additional circuitry, which was thought to be beyond the scope here.

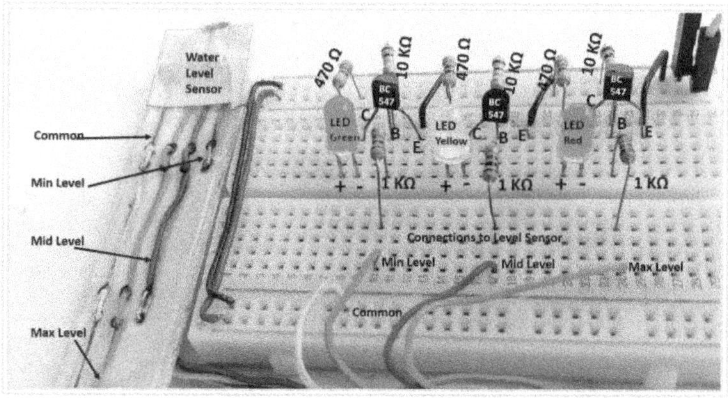

Fig – Component Layout on the breadboard

Now, if we gradually drain the water, we will observe the green LED turning off as the water level decreases below the full mark. Similarly, the Yellow & Red LEDs will turn off when the water level drops below the half /bottom level markings.

LED BLINKER USING IC 555

Let's begin our circuit exploration with a simple LED blinker circuit using one of the most widely known and simple Integrated Circuits (IC) – the NE555. This IC is popular among both circuit designers and hobbyists.

Circuit Diagram

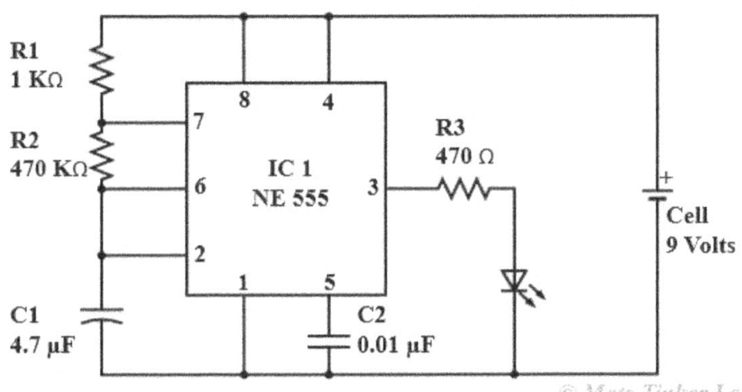

Components List

LED   *– 1 No*   *IC NE 555*   *– 1 No*
Capacitor 4.7 µF   *– 1 No*   *Capacitor 0.01 µF – 1 No*
Resistors 470 Ω, 1 K, 470 K – 1 Each

The IC will operate in a Free-running (Astable) mode, where the output oscillates between two voltage levels: high (a positive voltage) and low (ground or negative voltage). The LED, connected at the output, will continuously turn on (when output is high) and off (when output is low). The frequency of the output waveform (i.e., the speed at which the LED's on/off cycle repeats) and the duration of LED on/off can be controlled by selecting appropriate values for R1, R2 and C1. Increasing the value of R1, R2, or C1 will increase the time period of the output waveform and decreasing the value will decrease the time period.

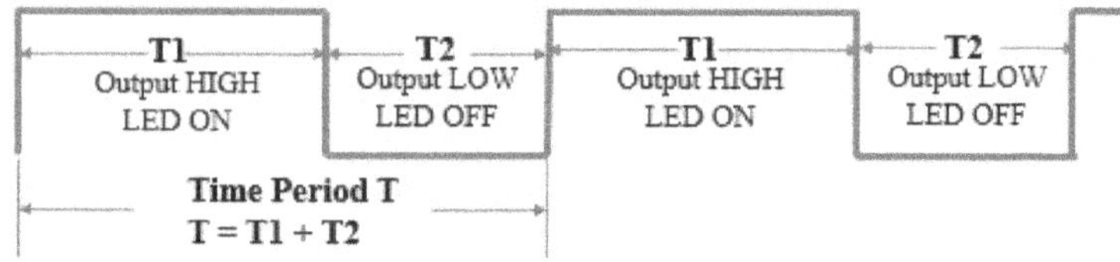

We can calculate the T1, T2 and the total time period T as shown below:

$$\textit{Time LED ON (T1)} = 0.693 \; x \; (R1+R2) \; x \; C1$$
$$\textit{Time LED OFF (T2)} = 0.693 \; x \; R2 \; x \; C1$$
$$\textit{Time Period (T)} = T1 + T2 \; seconds$$
$$\textit{Frequency (f)} = 1/T \; Hertz$$

R1 and R2 will be in Ohms and C1 in farads.
Time T1, T2 and T will be in seconds.

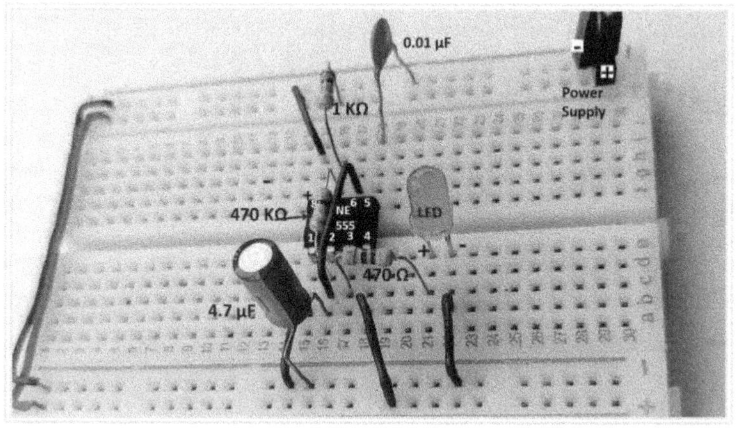

Fig – Component Layout on the breadboard

In our circuit, the time period T1 and T2 will be approximately 1.5 seconds. This means the LED will be turn on/off alternately at every 1.5 seconds.

<u>LED FADER</u>

In the blinker circuit that we just discussed, the LED turns on and off instantaneously. It would be interesting to add a 'fading in' and 'fading out' effect.

Circuit Diagram

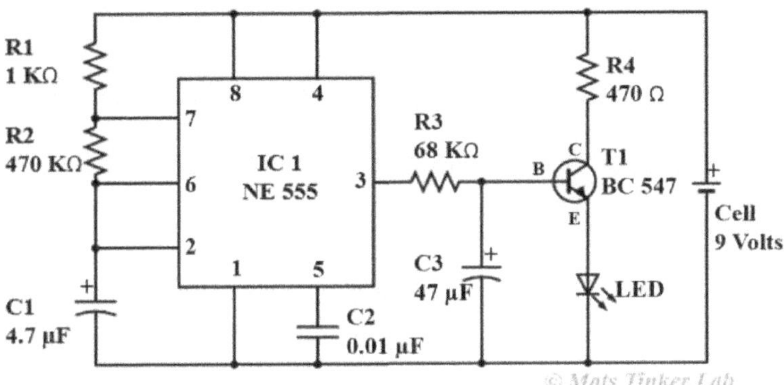

Components List

LED	*– 1 No*	*IC NE 555*	*– 1 No*
Transistor BC 547	*– 1 No*	*Capacitor 0.01 µF*	*– 1 No*
Capacitor 4.7 µF, 47 µF	*– 1 Ea*	*Resistors 470 Ω, 1 K*	*– 1 Ea*
Resistors 68K, 470 K	*– 1 Ea*		

The circuit is essentially the same, except for the output side. The output from Pin 3 is fed through a resistor (R3) and capacitor (C3) pair to the base of a transistor. The LED is connected at the emitter terminal of the transistor.

When the output at Pin 3 is high, capacitor C3 will gradually charge to the output voltage through R3. Consequently, the base voltage of the transistor will also smoothly increase. This will cause the transistor to provide a corresponding output that gradually rises from zero to the maximum value. As a result, the brightness of the LED gradually increases, providing a fading-in effect.

When the output voltage becomes zero (during T2), the capacitor gradually discharges through the 68 KΩ resistor. Consequently, the voltage at the base also gradually drops instead of changing quickly as seen in the blinker circuit. This gradual change causes the transistor output current to decrease gradually to zero as well. In effect, the brightness of the LED gradually diminishes, providing a fading effect.

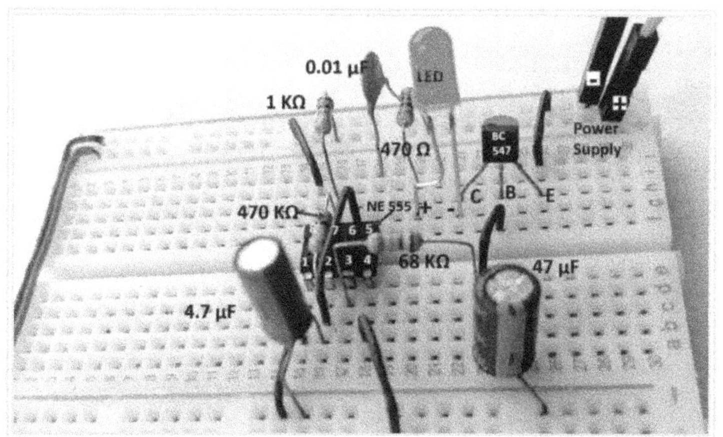

Fig – Component Layout on the breadboard

The fading In/fading Out time depends on the value of R3 and C3. Increasing the value of either will result in a longer time duration, and hence appear as a smoother fading In/fading Out.

LED FLASHER USING IC 555

Let us make a flasher by making a few changes at the output side in the blinker circuit. Add another 470 Ω resistor and LED at pin 3 of IC 555 to the previous circuit, as shown above.

Circuit Diagram

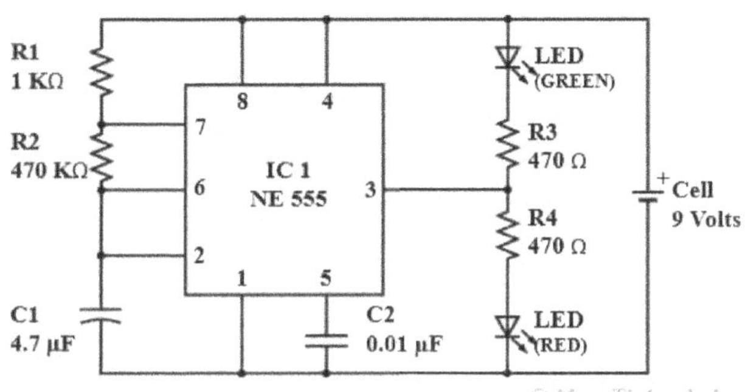

Components List

LED (Green/Red)	*– 1 Ea*	*IC NE 555*	*– 1 No*
Capacitor 4.7 µF	*– 1 No*	*Capacitor 0.01 µF*	*– 1 No*
Resistors 1 K, 470 K	*– 1 Ea*	*Resistor 470 Ω*	*– 2 Nos*

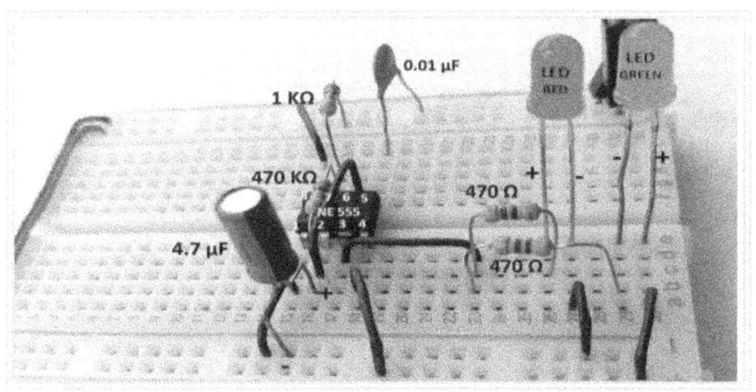

Fig – Component Layout on the breadboard

Both Red and Green LEDs will alternately turn on and off at every 1.5 seconds. The duration can be changed by changing R1 & R2 values.

TICK TOCK SOUND GENERATOR

Let's create a tiny circuit that makes sounds like a ticking time bomb from action movies! Such circuits are widely used in metronomes and digital clocks to give them that cool mechanical feel.

Circuit Diagram

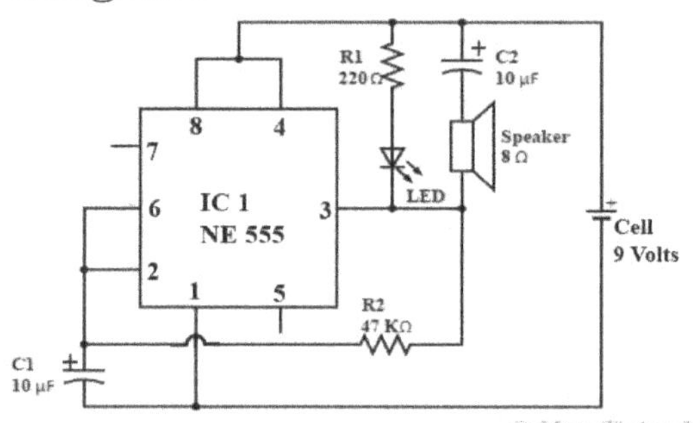

Components List

Loud Speaker 8 Ω, LED – 1 Ea   IC NE 555   – 1 No
Capacitor 10 µF   – 2 Nos   Resistors 220 Ω, 47K – 1 Ea

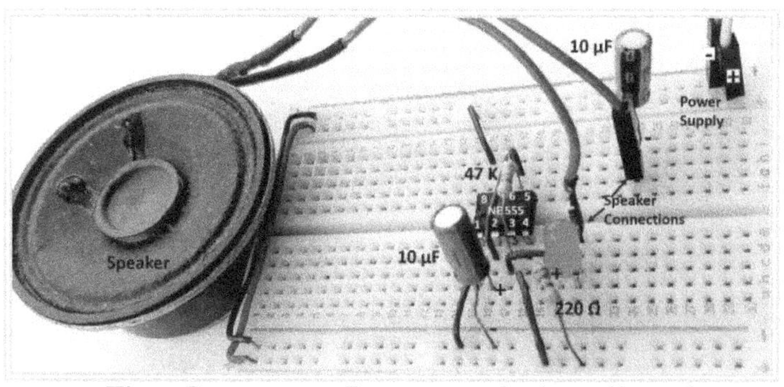

Fig – Component Layout on the breadboard

Output of the IC varies between low/ high states, at a frequency determined by R2/C1 combinations. During every transition from low to high and vice versa, the diaphragm of the speaker moves rapidly, which produces the Tick Tock sound.

ELECTRONIC MONO TONE SIREN

The electronic siren is a hobbyist's ticket to instant excitement! Here, we dive deep into the world of blaring horns, cacophonous chirps, and the sheer audacity of noise-making machines. Get ready to plug in your earplugs and crank up the volume because things are about to get hilariously loud!

Circuit Diagram

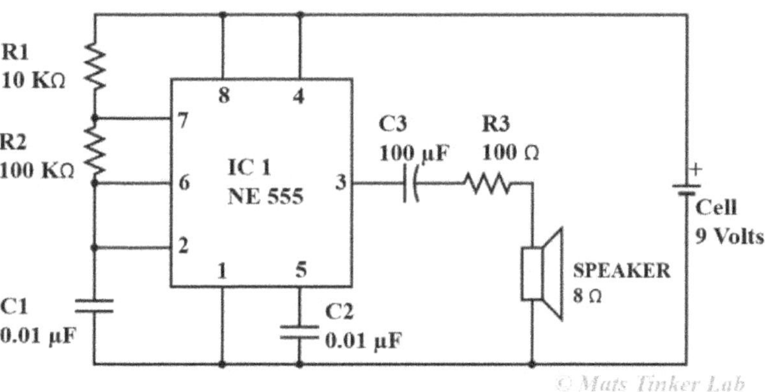

Components List

Loud Speaker 8 Ω	*– 1 No*	*IC NE 555*	*– 1 No*
Capacitor 0.01 µF	*– 2 Nos*	*Capacitor 100 µF*	*– 1 No*
Resistor 100 Ω	*– 1 No*	*Resistors 10 K, 100 K*	*– 1 Ea*

The IC 555 operates as an Astable multivibrator, producing a continuous oscillating signal, as demonstrated in the flashing LED circuit. The resistors R1 & R2, along with capacitor C1, determine the output signal frequency. In this configuration, the circuit generates an oscillating signal at 800 Hz, which is then fed to the speaker, resulting in the production of a high-pitched noise.

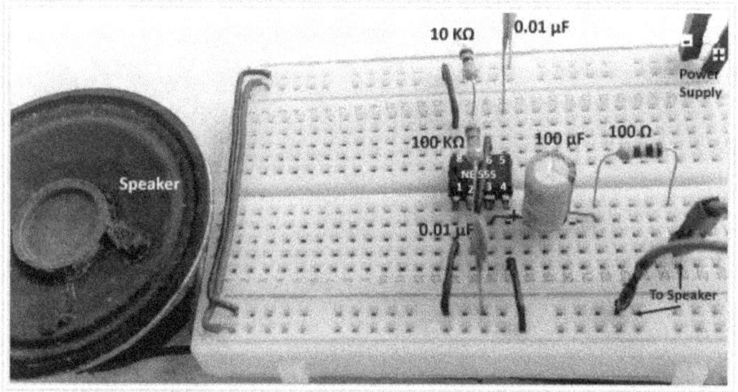

Fig – Component Layout on the breadboard

Replace the resistor R2 with a 10 K Ω resistor in series with a 100 KΩ potentiometer as shown in the schematic below.

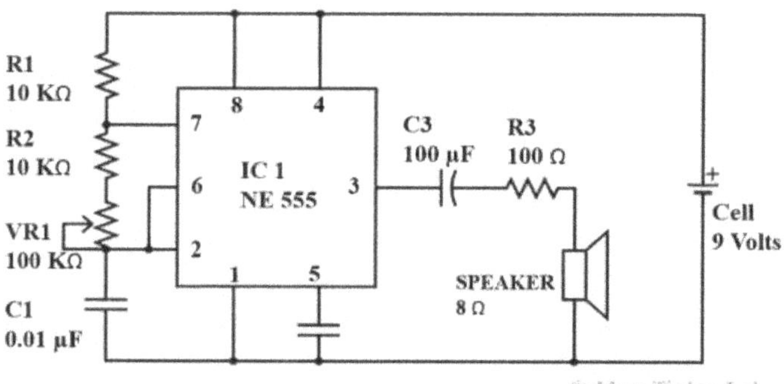

We can change the frequency of the output pulse by varying the resistance at the input side. This can be achieved by adjusting the slider of Potentiometer with a screw driver. In effect this will change the frequency of the output pulse, which can be felt from the pitch of the monotone noise originating from the speaker.

WAILING SOUND GENERATOR

Ever stopped to listen to the siren wailing from factories? It starts soft, grows to a thunderous peak, then gradually fades away, leaving only echoes in its wake. Fascinating, isn't it? Well, get ready to dive into the world of industrial soundscapes, because here, we're about to create a circuit that mimics the mighty roar of a factory siren!

Circuit Diagram

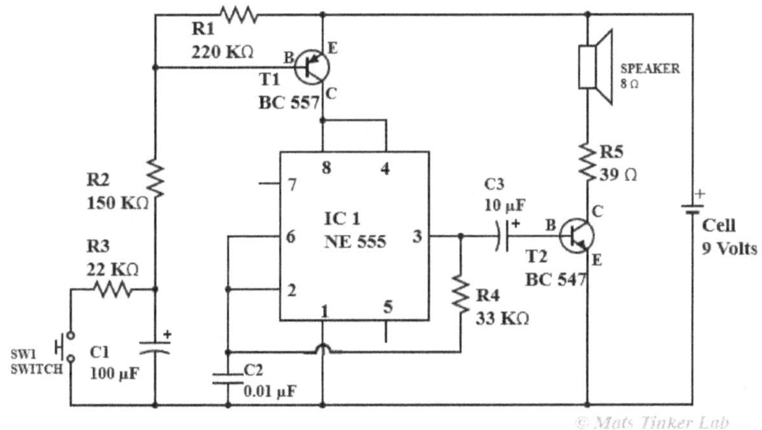

Components List

Loud Speaker 8 Ω	*– 1 No*	*IC NE 555*	*– 1 No*
Transistor BC 547/BC 557	*– 1 Ea*	*Capacitor 0.01µF*	*– 1 No*
Capacitor 10 µF, 100 µF	*– 1 Ea*	*Push Switch*	*– 1 No*
Resistors 39 Ω, 22 KΩ, 33 KΩ, 150 KΩ, 220 KΩ		*– 1 Each*	

The IC 555 operates in the astable multivibrator mode, producing audio at a fixed frequency. The transistor BC 557 is employed to supply power to the IC, regulating the current flowing through it and consequently controlling the intensity of its output.

When the switch SW1 is pressed, a negative voltage is delivered to the base of the transistor, causing it to switch on. As a result, the output current gradually rises to a peak level, mirroring the effect on the output of the IC and thus amplifying the intensity of the audio signal.

When the switch is released, the capacitor enters the charging state, drawing current through resistors R1 & R2. During this process, the base voltage of the transistor slowly rises from negative to positive, resulting in a gradual reduction of the output current. This change is also observed in the IC 555, causing its output to slowly fade out.

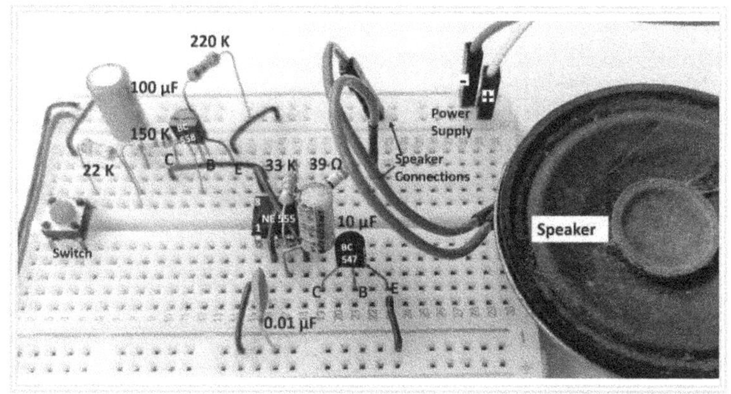

Fig – Component Layout on the breadboard

The sound produced by the speaker resembles that of a factory siren. Pressing the switch again causes the capacitor to discharge rapidly through resistor R3, promptly activating the transistor and reinitiating the wailing siren.

LIGHT SCREAMER

Let us make our alarm sensitive to light using a LDR. When there's no light, the alarm stays silent, but the moment light falls on the LDR, it springs to life! And here's the twist: the more the light, the louder the alarm gets! Imagine using this as your morning wake-up up alarm and see the fun!

Circuit Diagram

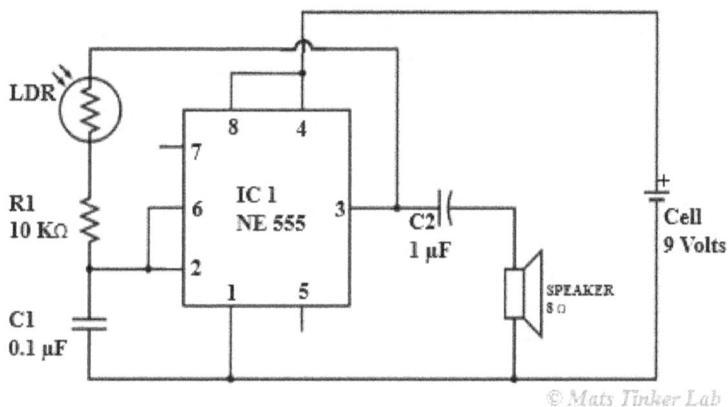

Components List

Loud Speaker 8 Ω	*– 1 No*	*IC NE 555*	*– 1 No*
Capacitor 0.1µF, 1 µF	*– 1 Ea*	*LDR 4.7 KΩ*	*– 1 No*
Resistor 10 KΩ	*– 1 No*		

We have already seen that changing the value of charging resistance, through which the capacitor charges and discharges, will change the output frequency. An increase in resistance value will result in a decrease in the frequency ($f = 1/T$) and a decrease in the resistance value results in a higher frequency of the generated tone.

In the screamer circuit here, the capacitor charges and discharges through the resistance R1, LDR and the output pin 3 of the IC.

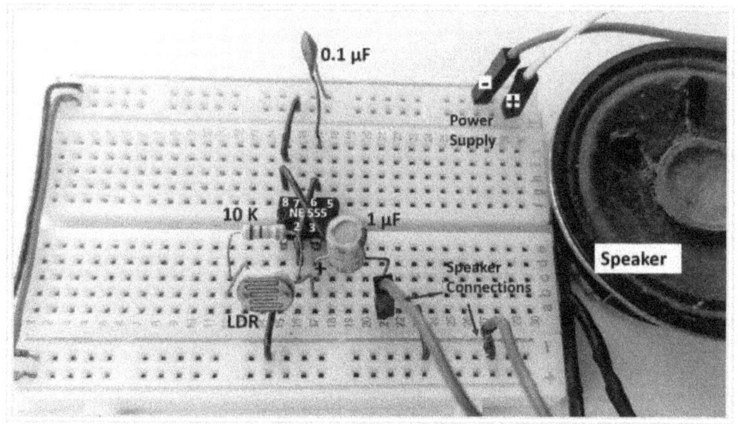

Fig – Component Layout on the breadboard

When it is pitch dark, no light falls on the LDR and therefore it offers maximum resistance. The frequency of the output signal will be low. The audio output will not be audible.

As the light intensity increases, the resistance of the LDR decreases, that further results in an increased frequency of the output signal. This produces a high pitched tone through the speaker.

When the light intensity reduces, the resistance increases and the output frequency reduces, giving a low pitched tone through the speakers.

In effect the pitch of the audio signal will correspond to the amount of light that falls up on the LDR.

TOUCH SWITCH

Let us now make the mundane task of turning on and off gadgets transforms into a magical touch! We've all encountered the traditional tumbler switches at home, but touch switches take it to a whole new level of excitement. No more loud clicking sounds or fumbling in the dark – just a gentle touch on the pad and the light comes on.

Circuit Diagram

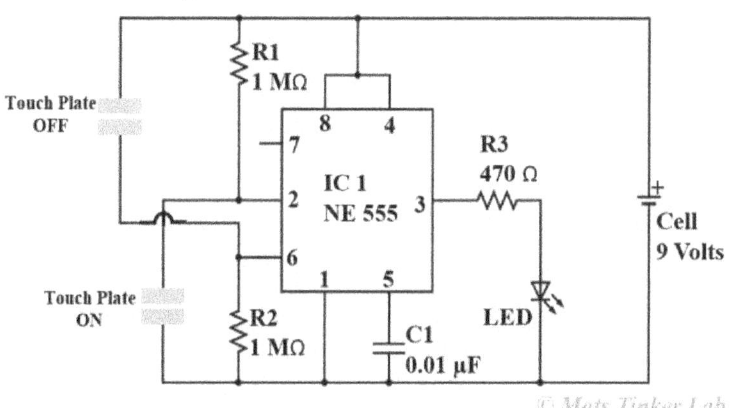

Components List

IC NE 555	– 1 No	LED	– 1 No
Capacitor 0.01 µF	– 1 No	Resistor 1 MΩ	– 2 Nos
Resistors 330 Ω	– 1 No	Touch pads	– 2 Nos

In the circuit we are utilizing the two sensing pins of NE 555 – the trigger pin (Pin 2) and the threshold pin (Pin 6). If the trigger pin detects any voltage less than 1/3 rd of the applied voltage, the output will be set to high. So, if pin 2 receives a voltage less than 3 volts, Pin 3 will go high, switching on the LED.

Similarly, if threshold pin detects any voltage greater than 2/3 rd of the applied voltage, the output will be set to low. That means, if a voltage greater than 6 volts is applied at pin 6, the output will go low, powering off the LED.

In the circuit, we keep the output at a stable state by applying Pin 2 with a positive voltage (greater than 3 volts) and Pin 6 with a zero volts, by connecting them to 9 Volts and ground points, through two resistors. This ensure the output remains at a stable state of High or Low.

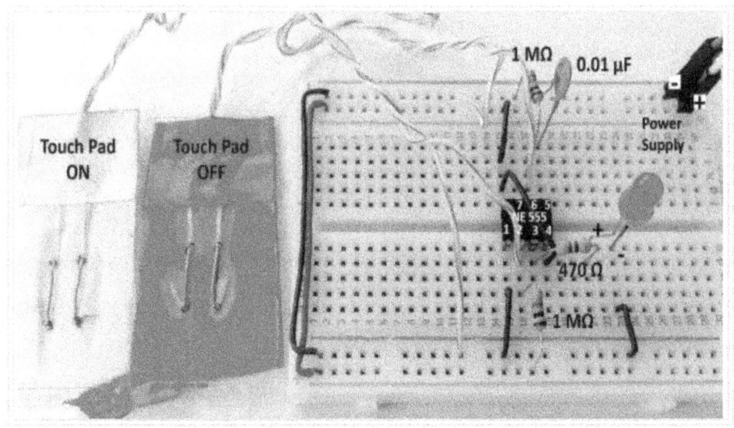

Fig – Component Layout on the breadboard

When the touch plate connected between Pin 2 and ground is touched, it senses a zero volt, and set the output to high. Now, if we touch the touch plate connected between Pin 6 and 9 volts, a positive voltage is sensed at Pin 6, and the output will be set to low.

FIVE MINUTES TIMER

Let us now step into the amazing world of timer circuits! They're like magic helpers in our daily routines. From making sure our microwave popcorn doesn't burn to turning on our favorite cartoons right on time, timer circuits are the secret behind all the cool stuff our gadgets can do!

Circuit Diagram

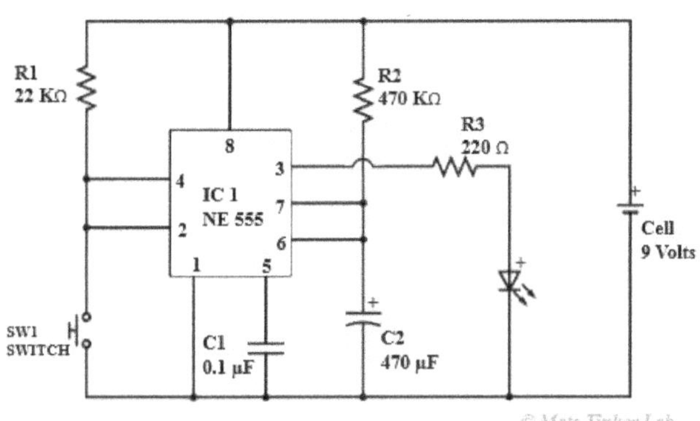

Components List

LED	*– 1 No*	*IC NE 555*	*– 1 No*
Capacitor 470 μF	*– 1 No*	*Capacitor 0.1 μF*	*– 1 No*
Resistors 220 Ω, 22 K, 470 K	*– 1 Ea*	*Push Switch*	*– 1 No*

In this circuit, the buzzer is connected between the positive supply and the output ping the IC. Hence, the buzzer remains off, if the output of the IC is high. The moment the output goes low, the buzzer triggers on.

Once the push switch SW1 is pressed and released, the timer starts. The output at pin 3 is set to high.

Charge starts building up across C2 through resistor R3. Once it is charged upto the threshold voltage, it triggers the output at pin 3 to low, thereby triggering the buzzer.

Fig – Component Layout on the breadboard

The delay offered in seconds is given by the formula Delay (in seconds) = 1.1*R3*C2, where the value of R3 is in Ohms and that of C2 in farads. For the given value of R2=470 KΩ and C2=470 µF, the delay will be around 5 minutes. We can increase the delay by increasing the value of resistor R2. For example, by replacing R2 with a 1 MΩ resistor, the timing can be increased to approximately 10 minutes.

LIGHT FENCE ALARM

Welcome aboard on an electrifying journey! In this adventure, we will combine the three components: the transistor, the Op Amp, and the timer chip NE555. Together, they form the backbone of a light fence circuit. It is a setup that detects movement by sensing the interruption of light beams, and springing an alarm into action, to raise an alert.

Circuit Diagram

Let's construct it in two parts. Firstly, we'll focus on the sensing mechanism and triggering a warning.

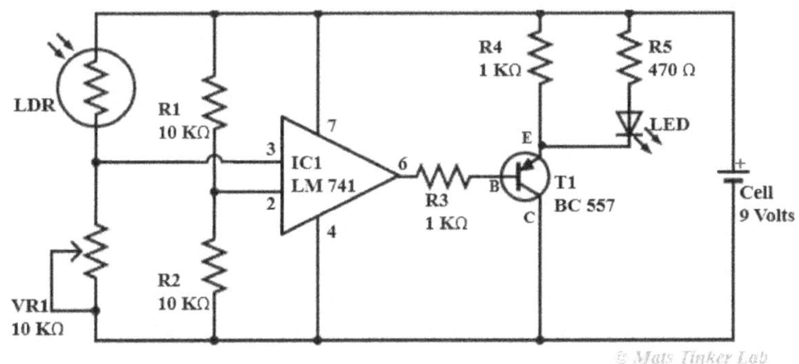

© Mats Tinker Lab

Components List

IC LM 741, NE 555	*– 1 Ea*	*Transistor BC 557*	*– 1 No*
LED, LDR	*– 1 Ea*	*Resistors 1 K, 10K*	*– 3 Nos*
Resistors 39 Ω, 470 Ω	*– 1 Ea*	*Resistors 10K*	*– 2 Nos*
Capacitors 0.1 µF, 10 µF	*– 1 Ea*	*Potentiometer 10 KΩ*	*– 1 No*

Pin 2 of IC 741 is biased to 4.5 volts via the two resistors R1 and R2. When desired amount of light is falling on the LDR, adjust the potentiometer VR1 to keep the alarm off. Now, if the light is obstructed by any means, LDR resistance increases, and the voltage at pin 3 of the IC becomes more negative. It leads to a low output at Pin 6 (Output), which activates the transistor T1, and triggers the LED.

We can expand the circuit with our second part that consists of an alarm circuit using IC 555.

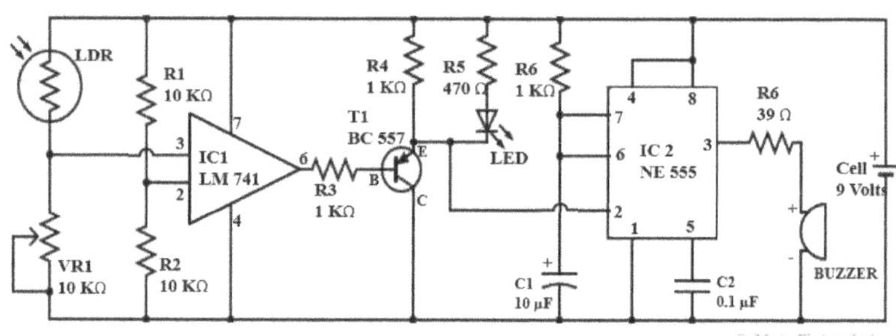

The output of the transistor (at the emitter pin) is connected to pin number 2 (Trigger pin) of IC 555, thereby triggering it into operation. The buzzer is triggered on, producing a high pitched audio warning, when an intrusion is detected.

Fig – Component Layout on the breadboard

CLAP SWITCH

Introducing the ultimate solution for those who prefer comfort over effort: the clap switch. If the mere thought of getting up to flip a switch leaves you exhausted, fear not – this innovative device is here to save the day. Imagine controlling your gadgets with just a simple clap, effortlessly replacing the need for traditional switches.

Circuit Diagram

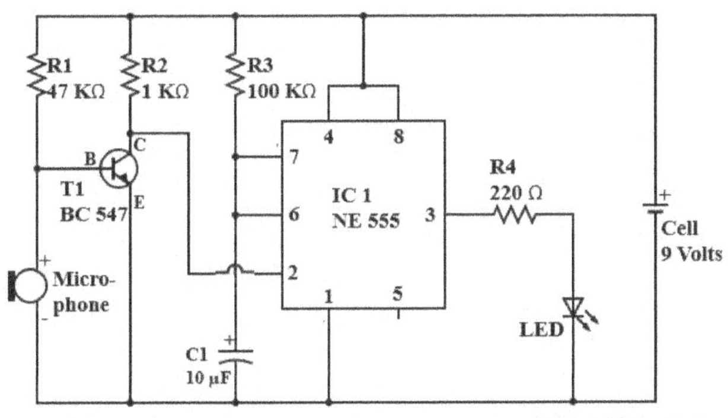

Components List

IC NE 555	*– 1 No*	*Transistor BC 547*	*– 1 No*
Condenser Mic	*– 1 No*	*LED*	*– 1 No*
Resistors 220 Ω, 1 K	*– 1 Ea*	*Resistors 47K, 100 K*	*– 1 Ea*
Capacitors 10 μF	*– 1 No*		

The microphone serves as the input device, transforming the clap sound into electrical signals. These signals drive transistor T1 into conduction, subsequently triggering IC 555. As a result, it generates a high output, powering on the LED. Upon removal of the audio input, the output reverts to a low voltage after a brief interval determined by the resistor (R3) and capacitor (C1) at the input side of the IC. In essence, the LED remains illuminated whenever the microphone detects an audio noise (such as a clap sound).

Latch Circuit

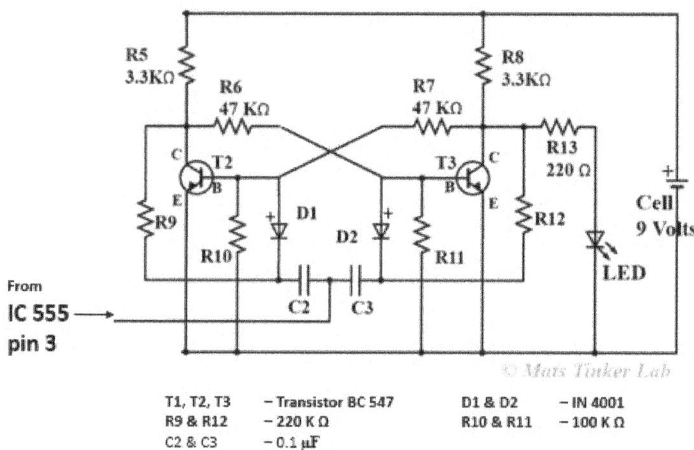

T1, T2, T3	– Transistor BC 547	D1 & D2	– IN 4001
R9 & R12	– 220 K Ω	R10 & R11	– 100 K Ω
C2 & C3	– 0.1 µF		

Additional Components List

Transistor BC 547	– 2 Nos	Diode 1N4001	– 2 Nos
Capacitors 0.1 µF	– 2 Nos	Resistors 3.3 K, 47 K	– 2 Ea
Resistors 220 Ω	– 1 No	Resistors 100 K, 220 K	– 2 Ea

In practice, the clap switch is designed to toggle a gadget on and off. To accomplish this, we incorporate a small circuit known as 'Latch circuit' at the output. A Latch circuit holds onto a high/low output state, regardless of any changes in the input. When the next pulse arrives (in this case, the next clap), it switches the output back to the other state. By integrating this circuit into the previous design, the first clap will activate the LED, and the subsequent clap will deactivate it.

The circuit shown above is indeed a Bistable multivibrator, triggered by a negative edge-triggered pulse. During bistable operation, one transistor (T2 or T3) conducts while the other (T3 or T2) remains off. When the negative edge trigger arrives at the base, the previously conducting transistor switches to cutoff state, simultaneously bringing the other into conduction. As a result, output shifts from high to low (or low to high).

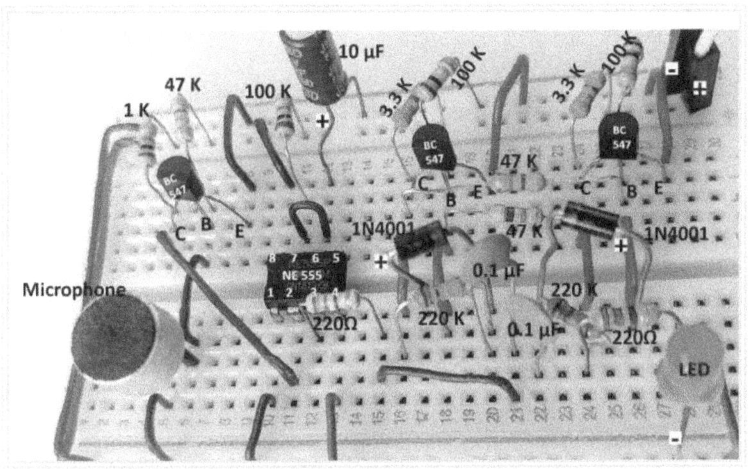

Fig – Component Layout on the breadboard

The combined circuit, integrating both the clap switch sensing circuit and the latch circuit, is depicted on the next page. It's crucial to exercise extreme care and planning when assembling numerous components on the breadboard to prevent mix-up and wiring errors. A recommended practice is to position the main components (such as ICs and transistors) in suitable locations and build the rest of the circuit around them.

R1 47 KΩ
R2 1 KΩ
T1
B C E
Micro-phone
C1 10 µF
R3 100 KΩ
IC 1 NE 555
4 8 7 6 2 C 3 1 5
R4 220 Ω
R5 3.3 KΩ
R6 47 KΩ
T2
C B E
R9
R10
D1
D2
C2
C3
R7 47 KΩ
T3
C B E
R11
R12
R8 3.3 KΩ
R13 220 Ω
LED
Cell 9 Volts
© Mats Tinker Lab
T1, T2, T3 – Transistor BC 547
R9 & R12 – 220 KΩ
C1 – 10 µF
D1 & D2 – IN 4001
R10 & R11 – 100 KΩ
C2 & C3 – 0.1 µF

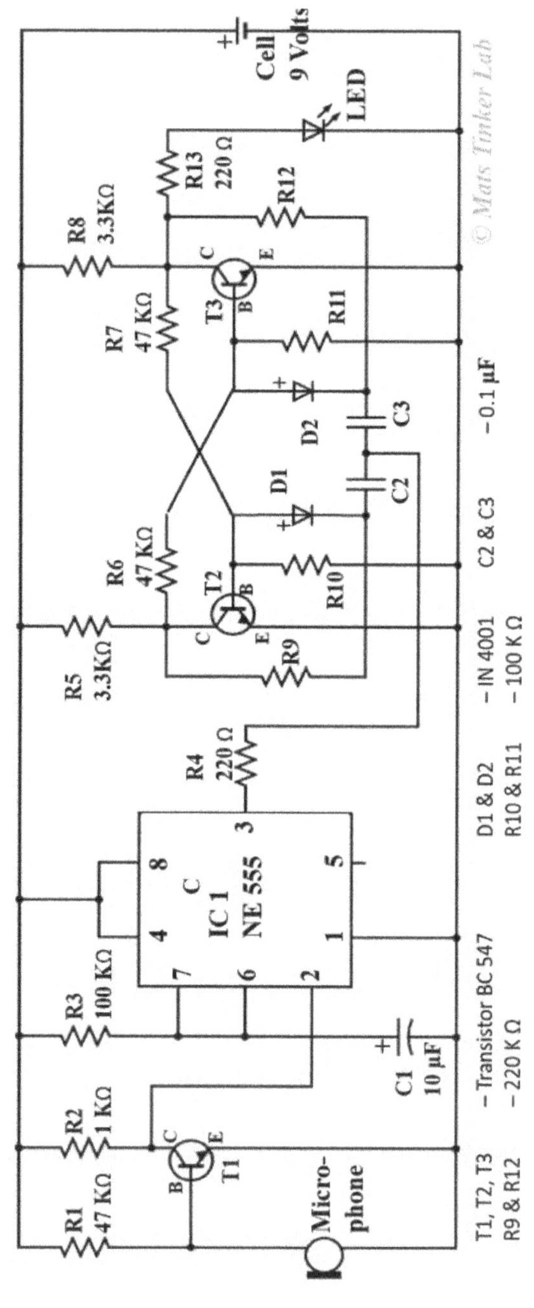

86

A SIMPLE AUDIO AMPLIFIER

Who doesn't dream of grabbing a microphone and belting out their favorite tunes for all to hear? It's the ultimate thrill! But to make those melodies truly shine, you need more than just a voice – you need a microphone and a circuit to amplify and rejuvenate that sound, making it loud and clear through the speaker. So, let's embark on an adventure to create a tiny yet powerful microphone amplifier, laying the foundation for endless musical moments and unforgettable performances!

Circuit Diagram

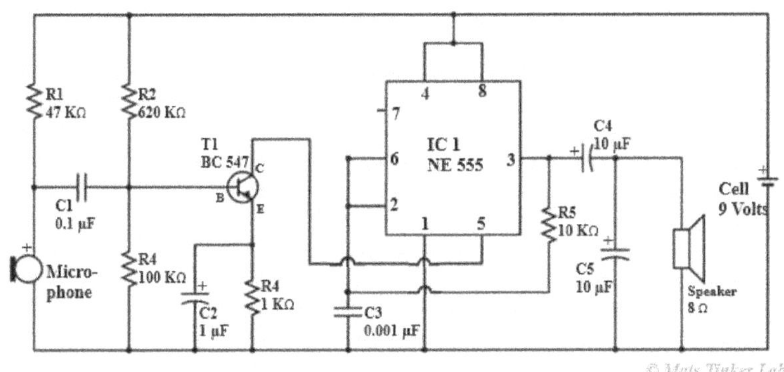

Components List

IC NE555	– 1 No	Transistor BC 547	– 1 No
Condenser Microphone	– 1 No	Loud Speaker 8 Ω	– 1 No
Capacitors 0.1 µF, 0.001 µF	– 1 Ea	Capacitor 1 µF	– 1 No
Capacitor 10 µF	– 2 Nos	Resistors 1 K, 10 K	– 1 Ea
Resistors 47 K, 100 K	– 1 Ea	Resistors 620 K	– 1 No

Any change in the voltage at Pin 5 of NE 555 will affect the width of the output pulse. If there's no input at Pin 5, the speaker will remain silent.

When the microphone detects audio, it transforms these sounds into electrical signals, which are then transmitted to Pin 5 via the transistor. This fluctuation in voltage leads to adjustments in the output pulse, ultimately translating into an audio signal reproduced by the speaker.

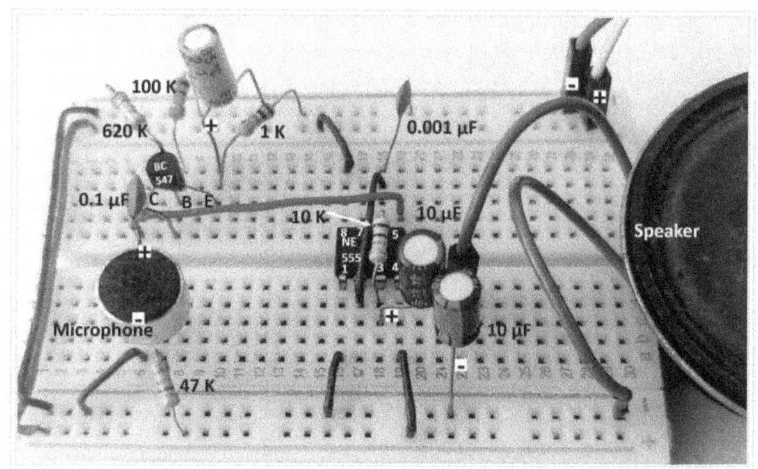

Fig – Component Layout on the breadboard

This audio amplifier circuit shown above is very basic and built around the components in the kit, to give the student an experience of making something new. The amplification provided will be very minimal, and hence the same may not be useful for any practical purpose.

COMPONENTS IN THE KIT

Integrated Chips (ICs)		Resistors	
NE 555 Timer	2 Nos	39 Ω, 100 Ω	1 Ea
LM 741 Op Amp	1 No	220 Ω	2 Nos
Transistors		330 Ω	1 No
BC 547 NPN	3 Nos	470 Ω, 1 KΩ	3 Ea
BC 558 PNP	1 No	3.3 KΩ, 4.7 KΩ	2 Ea
BC 557 PNP	1 No	10 KΩ	3 Ea
LEDs 5mm		22 KΩ, 33 KΩ	1 Ea
Red, Green, Yellow	1 Ea	47 KΩ	3 Nos
Capacitors (Polarized)		68 KΩ	1 No
1 µF, 16 Volts	1 No	100 KΩ	3 Nos
4.7 µF, 16 Volts	1 No	150 KΩ	1 No
10 µF, 16 Volts	2 Nos	220 KΩ	2 Nos
z47 µF, 16 Volts	2 Nos	470 KΩ, 620 KΩ	1 Ea
100 µF, 16 Volts	1 No	1 MΩ, 2.2 MΩ	2 Ea
220 µF, 16 Volts	1 No	**Sensors**	
470 µF, 16 Volts	1 No	LDR 47 KΩ	1 No
Capacitors (Un Polarized)		Thermistor 10K NTC	1 No
0.1 µF	2 No	IR Tx – Rx Pair	1 No
0.01 µF , 0.001 µF	1 Ea	**Other Items**	
Diodes		Battery Clip for 9V cell	1 No
IN 4001	2 Nos	Breadboard (Half Size)	1 No
Audio Devices		Push Switch	2 Nos
Condenser Microphone	1 No	Jumper (Male to Male)	15 Nos
Loud Speaker 8 Ω	1 No	Jumper (Male to Female)	5 Nos
Buzzer 9 Volts	1 No	Breadboard Wire 22 SWG	3 Mtrs
Potentiometer			
10 K, 47K, 100 K, 1 M	1 Ea		

Items Not Included in the Kit
- 9 Volt Cell (To be purchased locally)
- Touch Plates, Moisture Sensor (Plant Watering), Water Level Sensor and Rain Sensor. You are advised to make these sensors on your own, following the guidelines given in the book.
- Use the 22 SWG wire for making the sensors and short jumpers that are required to be used on the breadboard.

COMPONENT CODES

Resistors

Value	Picture	Colour Code
39 Ω		Orange, White, Black
100 Ω		Brown, Black, Brown
220 Ω		Red, Red, Brown
330 Ω		Orange, Orange, Brown
470 Ω		Yellow, Violet, Brown
1 K Ω		Brown, Black, Red
3.3 K Ω		Orange, Orange, Red
4.7 K Ω		Yellow, Violet, Red
10 K Ω		Brown, Black, Orange
22 K Ω		Red, Red, Orange
33 K Ω		Orange, Orange, Orange
47 K Ω		Yellow, Violet, Orange
68 K Ω		Blue, Grey, Orange
100 K Ω		Brown, Black, Yellow
150 K Ω		Brown, Green, Yellow
220 K Ω		Red, Red, Yellow
470 K Ω		Yellow, Violet, Yellow
620 K Ω		Blue, Red, Yellow
1 M Ω		Brown, Black, Green
2.2 M Ω		Red, Red, Green

Non-Polarized Capacitors

Value	Code
0.001 µF	102
0.01 µF	103
0.1 µF	104

TROUBLE SHOOTING

If you find something is missing or not working please follow the steps below:

- ➤ Check the polarity of power supply.
- ➤ Recheck if all the wiring has been done as per the circuit diagram.
- ➤ Check if the pins of ICs and transistors are connected correctly.
- ➤ Check if any of the pins/wires are inadvertently touching the nearby components or wires, resulting in a short.
- ➤ Check if the polarity of polarized capacitors, LED, Diode, Buzzer, IR Tx– Rx etc are correct.
- ➤ Check none of the components/ wires are loosely fitted in the holes on the breadboard.
- ➤ If the lower half of the breadboard is used, ensure that the power rails of both halves are interconnected with jumpers.
- ➤ Check if the battery is drained out completely. You may use a new battery to verify this, after all the above steps have been thoroughly checked and verified.
- ➤ In none of this is solving your issue, please send a photo of your wired circuit to us via email, which we will check and revert to you with possible solutions.

Note: Wrong connection or improper handling of components could result in irrecoverable damage to the components.

GET ASSISTANCE

All videos showcasing the construction of every circuit would soon be available on our YouTube channel - @mats_lab.

If you want a softcopy of the Circuit Diagrams and the component layout diagrams (in colour) or have any further questions, feel free to reach out to us via our email ID - mats.learning@gmail.com.

Furthermore, component kits will soon be available on Amazon.in. Additionally, we are in the process of partnering with a few electronic component suppliers, which on completion will allow you to conveniently order kits through their portals.

For enthusiast's eager to dive into exploration without any delay, we offer direct supply of kits at an attractive price. To inquire further, kindly reach out to us via the mentioned email ID.

www.ingramcontent.com/pod-product-compliance
Lightning Source LLC
Chambersburg PA
CBHW040739120726
48007CB00008B/136